D1614288

STREETFIGHTING

STREETFIGHTING

Low-Cost Advertising/ Promotion Strategies for Your Small Business

Jeff Slutsky

Prentice-Hall, Inc.   Englewood Cliffs, New Jersey

Prentice-Hall International, Inc., *London*
Prentice-Hall of Australia, Pty. Ltd., *Sydney*
Prentice-Hall Canada, Inc., *Toronto*
Prentice-Hall of India Private Ltd., *New Delhi*
Prentice-Hall of Japan, Inc., *Tokyo*
Prentice-Hall of Southeast Asia Pte. Ltd., *Singapore*
Whitehall Books, Ltd., *Wellington, New Zealand*
Editora Prentice-Hall do Brasil Ltda., *Rio de Janeiro*

© 1984 by
Prentice-Hall, Inc.
Englewood Cliffs, N.J.

Library of Congress Cataloging in Publication Data
Slutsky, Jeff,
    Streetfighting: Low-cost advertising/promotion
strategies for your small business.

    Includes index.
    1. Advertising.   2. Sales promotion.   3. Small
business. I. Woodruff, Woody. II. Title.
HF5823.S614   1984   659.1   83-13806
ISBN 0-13-851550-6
ISBN 0-13-851543-3 {PBK}

10 9 8 7 6 5 4 3 2

Printed in the United States of America

Preface

Streetfighting is really an attitude.

An attitude which is best summed up by the small business owner who one day realizes this simple fact: "I can't *outspend* my competition. Therefore, I must outsmart them!"

And while this attitude can certainly be applied to many areas of running a small business, this book deals specifically with perhaps one of the most mystifying areas to many an otherwise successful entrepreneur—that of advertising and sales promotion.

Our intent, however, is to demystify this process for you. To write in simple, understandable language. To guide you through the principles we have come to call *streetfighting.* To help you stretch your minds as much as we help you stretch your advertising budget—and most of all, to instill in you the attitude of streetfighting.

Prior to developing this attitude, first in ourselves and then for our clients, we did our share of conventional advertising. Within the advertising agencies we worked for, we created and placed our clients' ads in newspapers, radio, television, and outdoor media.

Then several years ago, we noticed something: It simply wasn't working as well as it once did. Our clients still got results—but not as much and not as often.

In short, the media had begun to self-destruct.

Rather than go back and ask our clients to spend more money on advertising, which seemed to be the accepted practice of the day, we began to question traditional advertising methods. We also invented new ones, tested them for results, fine-tuned them, tested them again, and made them better yet.

Out of all this trial and error testing came several things. First was the formation of the Retail Marketing Institute, the publication of our monthly newsletter, *Streetfighter*™ and our original seminar, The Streetfighter's Guide to Media Alternatives. In it, we taught our attendees how to get free distribution of their advertising message, along with hundreds of other low-cost but cost-effective ways to generate sales!

It worked! Our attendees reported substantially increased sales by using streetfighting methods.

Yet it wasn't enough. Even applying every streetfighting technique in the book, it became clear to us that some selective use of mass media was still necessary. So we asked ourselves if some of these same techniques could be applied to radio, TV, newspapers, and billboards.

From our agency backgrounds, we already knew that most broadcast rate cards were made of rubber, and the ones published by newspapers were etched in stone. Yet there had to be ways to get more for those mass media dollars. A lot more!

We also knew that our theory about the media beginning to self-destruct was becoming more and more a factor. Newspaper costs continued to rise despite declining readership. Rates soared in television even though the prime-time network viewing share had dropped from 95 percent in 1977 to an estimated 77 percent in 1982. Radio rates skyrocketed in the face of eroding station loyalty—too many stations, too many commercials, and too much button punching.

Yet all was not lost! One of our methods was best summarized in a line from the movie *Godfather II*. At one point, Michael Corleone remembers a piece of advice his father once gave him: "Keep your friends close, but your enemies closer." That's exactly what we began to do. *The media were the enemy.* Our job was to get closer to them.

So we became close. We learned everything we could from them. From the newest sales rep on the street to the seasoned pros in top management. We learned how they functioned internally, what the motivations of the various people were, where the problems were, and what the opportunities were. We discovered what it takes to get the most from the mass media. In short, the ability to sell the salesperson, read the rating books, punch the program director's hot button, and negotiate with the noble, the naive, the narrow-minded, and the numbskull!

Thus, the circle was complete. First, the search for mass media alternatives for small and medium-sized business. Then the search for ways to apply the same principles to the mass media itself. Looking back, it was all a matter of attitude—the development of the streetfighter's attitude toward advertising and sales promotions.

It's the attitude that shaped the techniques contained in this book. The programs described in the following pages are not just theories—they have been implemented by a growing variety of retailers throughout the world. You can do it, too!

It won't be easy. We offer no simple answers, magic wands, or silver bullets. It will take hard work, but you can do it; furthermore, you MUST do it if you are to survive the years ahead. So become a streetfighter, develop the attitude, then you can do anything! Welcome aboard!

Jeff Slutsky

CONTENTS

CHAPTER 3
COMMUNITY INVOLVEMENT AND YOUR BOTTOM LINE 60

CHAPTER 4
IN-STORE MARKETING 86

CHAPTER 5
OFF-PREMISES PROMOTIONS 110

CHAPTER 6
STREETSMART DIRECT MAIL 122

CHAPTER 7
RADIO: RED-HOT OR RIP-OFF?. 146

CHAPTER 10
THE GREAT OUTDOORS! IS IT REALLY SO GREAT? 208

CHAPTER 11
EYES OPEN, EARS TO THE GROUND. 220

1

CROSS-PROMOTIONS— THE FREE FORM OF ADVERTISING

That's right, free. As in costing zip or no charge. *Spending* "negabucks," as opposed to *wasting.* "megabucks." Getting your advertising free is a new concept to most business people, but it forms the foundation of the streetfighter's mentality toward effective marketing.

The power of the cross-promotion was certainly understood some 200 years ago when used by Benjamin Franklin. In some of his earlier editions of *Poor Richard's Almanac,* readers could take advantage of valuable coupons from various merchants of the day, including a sizable savings from Paul Revere's Silver and Pewter Shop. It might very well have been the first "two for one," (two if by sea, of course). Ben evidently felt that discount coupons added to the value of his publication, making it easier for him to sell—and Paul was none the worse for this cooperative merchandising either. It sure beat the hell out of riding horseback through the streets yelling, "My stock liquidation sale is coming . . . my sale is coming!" (And, in honor of Benjamin Franklin and Paul Revere, and in keeping with the philosophy that we practice what we preach, you'll find in the back of this book a valuable coupon entitling you to a free gift when you subscribe to our newsletter, *Streetfighter.)*

As you can tell from this brief history lesson, we did not invent the cross-promotion. We never claimed that we did. We do feel that we have greatly improved this concept and adapted it to be very effective in today's market. This wasn't an overnight occurrence either. Many years were spent testing, experimenting, making small improvements every step of the way.

15

As a streetfighter, you will learn that there's little new under the sun. Don't try to reinvent the wheel, but rather, *look for small improvements on existing successful programs.* You can't put bread on the table with advertising awards from well-produced commercials or brochures unless they generate sales. So if you see a technique, promotion, idea, or concept that worked for someone else, steal it! Actually, we prefer to use the term *creative borrowing.* If you really want to get technical, it's usually called stealing if you discovered the idea from one source. If you find it from two sources, then you call it *research.*

Regardless of whether you steal it, research it, or borrow it, the trick is to be able to identify those elements of a given promotion or concept that can be extracted, adapted, and improved to work in your situation.

In this chapter you will learn about a number of successful cross-promotions, and some not so successful. You'll learn what worked, what didn't work, and why. As far as we're concerned, the best cross-promotions haven't been done yet. That'll be up to you.

We first started using cross-promotions for clients in the food service and entertainment fields. After developing a good track record with these alternative advertising methods, many other types of businesses asked if these techniques would work for them. We didn't know, but they allowed us to test, experiment, make a few mistakes, and then try our own small improvements. It worked. It worked for a number of different and unrelated businesses—from fitness centers to fabric shops, from carpeting stores to karate schools. The cross-promotions were intoxicating for nightclubs; they set a precedent for a legal clinic. Whether or not you can make them work for you will depend on your understanding of the streetfighting concepts forthcoming.

The Medium and the Message

Cross-promotions, like all forms of advertising, comprise two elements, the medium and the message. It's the media that the large portion of advertising budgets are devoted to. The reason is simple: It's the most expensive part of advertising. The media provide the means of distribution of the advertising message. The cost of producing a radio or TV commercial, or laying out a yellow page ad, newspaper ad, or direct mail piece, is a small fraction of what it costs to buy the time, space, or postage to get that message to the public.

With the cross-promotion we are able to combine an effective message and free distribution. In a sense, we have created our own advertising medium with no monthly bills. There's no newspaper space to buy or postage to pay. Cross-promotions are sometimes called "poor man's direct mail," a term not so richly deserved, for they have made many a merchant anything but poor. In our opinion, cross-promotions are truly one of the mass media alternatives that can deliver us through the 80s.

The Streetfighter Who Made $1,803 on a $40 Promotion

A Nautilus Fitness Center implemented one of the healthier cross-promotions that we discovered. In addition to their yearly membership of $300, they also provided a special introductory membership—three visits for $19.50. The primary purpose of the "intro" was to get people to try it out. They felt like they had a good opportunity to convert the "intro" into a regular membership once they got people in the front door.

To set up the cross-promotions, the Nautilus manager met with the owner of a tennis club. After introducing himself, he explained the benefits of the Nautilus program for tennis players. He showed the owner a magazine article featuring Arthur Ashe, Billy Jean King, and Chris Evert Lloyd using Nautilus to prevent tennis elbow and to help increase the power of their serves.

He then told the owner, "We would like to provide you with special half-price discount coupons for one introductory membership, compliments of the tennis club. You then provide them to your members as an added value. A little something extra for their membership fee." He then showed him a coupon similar to the one he would print for the tennis club, one that was done for another group. (See Figure 1-1.) The tennis club owner was intrigued by his proposal but had one question on his mind: "How much is it going to cost me?"

"That's the best part of this program," the Nautilus manager replied. "It costs you nothing! We even pay for the printing and paper."

For Our Members...
Discover Nautilus

COMPLIMENTS OF

Wildwood RACQUET CLUB

- Prevent Tennis Elbow
- Improve Power of Serve
- Develop Greater Stamina
- Increase Overall Strength
- Further Flexibility
- Control Weight

USE THIS VALUABLE COUPON TODAY!

NAUTILUS IS USED BY ARTHUR ASHE, BILLIE JEAN KING, CHRIS EVERT LLOYD. NOW YOU CAN TOO!

━━━━━━━━━━━ COUPON ━━━━━━━━━━━

SAVE 50%

ON THE REGULAR PRICE OF THE NAUTILUS INTRODUCTORY PROGRAM. YOU SAVE $9.75.

All Sports Fitness Center
3602 S. Calhoun (Across from South Side H.S.)
456-1956

ONLY ONE COUPON PER PERSON EXPIRES 5/31/81

Figure 1-1

The owner was excited. It turned out that the tennis club had a monthly newsletter that was mailed to their 1,000 members. The owner agreed to insert the coupons in the envelopes the next month. And since he had never been to the Nautilus center, the manager gave him a card like the one in Figure 1-2, entitling him to three free visits.

The 1,000 coupons were distributed the following month and eight of them were redeemed, which brought in $87. Of those eight intros, five were converted to one-year memberships and one to a six-month membership. The gross sales for the promotion totaled $1,803. The cost of production was a whopping $40!

Over a period of time, this manager was responsible for a number of other cross-promotions. Not all of them worked as well as did the

FREE PASS

ALL SPORTS
NAUTILUS FITNESS CENTER

THIS PASS ENTITLES THE BEARER
TO THREE FREE VISITS.

Authorized by_____

Offer Expires____/____/____

3602 SOUTH CALHOUN (Across from South Side) • (219) 456-1956
OPEN SIX DAYS A WEEK • CALL FOR AN APPOINTMENT

Figure 1-2

tennis club coupon; some didn't work at all. The cost was so low, however, and the returns so potentially high, that he could afford a few mistakes. Something you can't afford to do with megabucks in the mass media.

This sample cross-promotion scenario may sound painfully simple. It isn't. A close look at all the subtleties involved will reveal that it's a very complex marketing tool. A tool with a very low tolerance for abuse. Implemented improperly it can cause some major grief. A careless cross-promotion can even put you out of business. On the other hand, when implemented properly it can increase your profits enormously. It's very much like the Japanese fugu fish, a delicacy in Japan. It's a poisonous fish and must be prepared by specially licensed chefs. With a mistake in the preparation it can be deadly, but prepared properly, it is the finest dining experience. You, too, must be specially trained so that you may prepare the finest of streetfighting delicacies, the cross-promotion. Your training begins with "The Three Cs."

The Three Cs of Cross-Promotions

The three Cs of cross-promotions are cost, control, and credibility. All three are important. Each C provides a special dimension to the concept that allows you the absolute maximum flexibility and return on investment.

Cost

In the story of the Nautilus Fitness Center, the manager was able to get 1,000 coupons distributed free. The only cost he had was the printing of the coupons, and that was very inexpensive printing from his local quick printer.

Why would other people be willing to pass out your advertising for you, free? They wouldn't ... unless there's something in it for them. If the Nautilus manager said to the tennis club owner, "We'd like you to pass out these coupons for us," he probably would have been told what to do with his coupons. The owner would not have seen any benefit for himself. Therefore, you must create a value for your cross-promotion partner, a perceived value for the recipient.

The Nautilus manager supplied the owner of the tennis club with

1,000 coupons, $40 worth of printing. It was not perceived by the tennis club owner as $40 worth of printing, but $9,750 worth of valuable savings for his members. Obviously, the Nautilus manager wasn't giving up thousands of dollars, yet the owner perceived it as such.

The success of getting your advertising distributed free depends on your ability to present the value of the program to your partner, to stress the *you* benefits. "We're providing *you* with these coupons to provide to *your* customers, at no cost to *you*."

Probably the ultimate example of the effective use of perceived value was done by a former seminar attendee who owns a multiunit food service operation in the South. He approached a threeunit grocery store business about a cross-promotion. He explained the entire program very carefully, stressing the *you* benefits and building the perceived value as high as possible. The grocery owners were excited, very excited. They had only one question, "How much?"

He thought for a brief moment and then replied, "$1,000." They agreed! It was the most amazing thing we had ever heard.

However, we don't recommend that you try this. To actually ask somebody to pay you to distribute your coupons or fliers is an advanced, gutsy level of streetfighting that would take many years to master. Please keep in mind that your goal is to get free distribution for your advertising. That in itself is remarkable, but knowing that some people would be willing to pay for it should be encouraging to you.

Control

When using your local newspaper or tabloid, you have very little control over your advertising. You can't control how many messages go out, where they go, or who gets them.

For the most part, using the mass media means that your advertising goes out to the masses, but your customer base may be a very specific type or group of people. With the cross-promotion you have numeric, geographic, and demographic control.

Numeric Control

If your local newspaper has a circulation of 30,000 and you place a coupon in it, like the one in Figure 1-3, you have to distribute

```
Compliments of MedPAC
The bearer of this card is entitled to a free legal consultation valued at $10.00 from
Trotter
    Rothberg
         Chambers
            LEGAL CLINIC
Stoney Creek Professional Village on Washington Center Road
6079 Stoney Creek Drive                    (219) 484-4114
Next to the Marriott                  Only One Coupon Per Person
           Expires February 15, 1982
```

Figure 1-3

30,000 coupons. You are forced to distribute as many coupons as issues of publication you're using. Many times that might be too much exposure. During an off time, you may want to distribute a "high-liability" coupon to generate sales. A high-liability discount is one that is very high in savings. It is purposely high to ensure its redemption to build traffic. A high-liability discount may be a two-for-one, 50 percent off, or even free merchandise. With this kind of heavy discounting, you may not be able to handle all of the business if the coupons go out to 30,000 homes. Generally, the higher the discount, the higher the redemption.

When you're dealing with a limited amount of merchandise or can handle only a limited number of customers, the numeric control can keep you from upsetting customers because you ran out of the item or they waited too long.

With the cross-promotion you can limit the number of coupons you distribute. If the weekly customer count of your promotion partner is 15,000 and you want to pass out only 5,000 coupons, you provide only 5,000 coupons. Distribution can be limited to two or three days, or until all the coupons have been distributed.

Geographic Control

Even though some publications have zones that allow you to section off part of your distribution, you still have your advertising reaching a large area. For the most part, retail businesses receive the majority of their customers from an area anywhere from a five- to six-block radius, to a two- or three-mile radius from their location. There are exceptions to this, but as a rule, the closer to your store the customers are, the higher chance of their shopping at your store.

With mass media you may be reaching many people who probably won't shop at your store. If you have a number of locations in the same city, the mass media become more important, but even then you will find it valuable to have more control as to where your advertising is exposed.

In Figure 1-4, you'll see that we've divided the area from which the customers are drawn into the primary and secondary service areas. For most retail outlets, the primary area directly surrounding the store is where the majority of the business will come from. The secondary area, further away, will attract less, but still a significant amount of business. A smaller percentage will come from various other areas.

In low-volume or new locations, you'll want to concentrate in that primary area, starting with those "people magnets" that are closest to your store, then moving outward. A "people magnet" is any

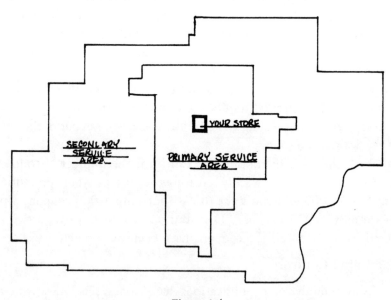

Figure 1-4

Figure 1-5

gathering place where a majority of your type of customers can be found (see Figure 1-5).

By conducting a cross-promotion in your own back yard, so to speak, you'll attract mostly people who would likely use your store as a result of convenience. By concentrating in your neighborhood, you avoid a lot of waste that you might get if you placed the same message in a newspaper.

Now let's assume that you have a well-established, high-volume store. The majority of your customers are coming from that primary service area, and you don't want to issue a discount in that area because you would be discounting your regular customers. They are already paying full price, so a coupon would be money out of your pocket.

Yet you could use a few more regular customers—who couldn't? In this situation, you concentrate your cross-promotion efforts with those merchants in that secondary service area. Granted, your redemption will be lower because you are less convenient to those people, but your chance of getting trial from a person who has never been to your store is very high.

Now let's assume you have three locations in town, and one is showing soft sales. A high-liability discount coupon in the newspaper might be overwhelming to your two high-volume locations and cause unneeded discounting. By concentrating your cross-promotion in the primary service area of the low-volume store, the vast majority of the coupons will be redeemed by the nearby location. You should experience only a minimal spill into the higher volume locations.

This is also a good concept to keep in mind when dealing with a competitor. By implementing cross-promotions in your competitor's primary service area, you are more likely to pick up a new customer and at the same time give your competition a harder way to go. Another side benefit of the cross-promotion is that it allows you a minimal amount of competitor awareness. With your coupon in the newspaper, your competition will know exactly what you're doing—which allows them an easier time to respond. With cross-promotions, though, you can do your damage quickly without ever letting them know what hit them until it's over . . . a little like guerrilla warfare.

Demographic Control

You may be able to target a little by placing your newspaper ad in various sections of the paper, but the price of your ad is based on the total circulation and not on what or who you want to reach. With a cross-promotion, you can work with those merchants or organizations that will attract the type of people you want for your customers. Demography is a classifying of people by their age, sex, income, likes, dislikes, etc. In the mass media you may be able to target by age and sex to some degree, but you still are reaching the masses and paying for it. However, this is not as likely with the cross-promotion. When the Nautilus Fitness Center manager worked with the tennis club, he was able to isolate a group of people that would have a need and be willing to pay $300 for a membership. When he set up a cross-promotion with a grocery store that distributed ten times as many coupons, he received less than half the responses. So you have the flexibility to target a specific group of people and gear your message specifically for them.

A restaurant may wish to work a cross-promotion with a movie theater because after the movie many people could be looking for a place to eat. On the other hand, people getting out of a movie probably wouldn't be interested in buying carpet, yet customers of a paint store might. Also, while customers of an office supply store may

1. **FREE TUXEDO** For the Groom
   (with 6 or more)

2. **FREE SHOES** For Everyone

3. **10 % off** an entire outfit for either:
   - Bride's father
   - Groom's father
   - Ring bearer

NORTH 3322 N. Anthony Blvd. **484-6824**
(North Anthony Shopping Center)

269 E. Coliseum Blvd. **482-8585**
(K-Mart Plaza North)

SOUTH 5909 Bluffton Road **747-4070**
(Wayne Plaza Shopping Center)

Courtesy of Armstrong's Diamond Center

Figure 1-6

not need paint, they probably are prime candidates for quick printing or dictation equipment.

To figure out where the prime people magnets are for your business, ask yourself: What other types of products and services would my customers need? Who would really need my products? People buying new suits and dresses would probably need dry cleaning. Young couples buying engagement rings probably could use some information about formal wear and floral arrangements (see Figure 1-6). Clients at a weight reducing clinic hope they will soon be in need of alterations and new clothes. Buyers of maternity dresses may soon be in the market for toys and baby clothes. Whether you're a family restaurant that needs to reach a general group through a grocery store or discount house, or a pet salon with a target group that may be reached more effectively by working with pet shops, cross-promotions can help you target those customers that can do you the most good. So start making a list of targeted people magnets for your business today.

Credibility

Even with all the features mentioned so far with the cross-promotions, perhaps the most interesting and beneficial is the aspect of credibility. This is also the most subtle of the three Cs, yet can be responsible for saving you thousands of dollars that might have forfeited due to overdiscounting or overcouponing.

When you advertise a discount or coupon in the newspaper, there is no doubt in any reader's mind that *you* are buying that space to discount *your* products. You are, in effect, telling the public that you are willing to give them a break in price. Your regular price becomes meaningless, since you are willfully disregarding it. People will respond to these ads, but if you coupon constantly, you may train your customers to expect a coupon all the time.

Some businesses are heavily into couponing. They mail four-color coupons to thousands of homes, and they run coupons in the newspaper, as well as four-color inserts. Because of this high volume of couponing, their customers come to expect the coupon. They may even refuse to go to a business because they forgot their coupons that day. The customers become less willing to pay the full price, and therefore the discounted price becomes the regular price.

Any business has to earn a certain amount of profit to make staying in the business worthwhile. When customers redeem a large number of coupons, that discount is reflected in the profit, and the regular prices are adjusted accordingly. It gets to the point, sometimes, that the customers may ask themselves, "Why don't they just cut their prices and save us all the trouble?" When it comes to that, the coupon is no longer effective. Furthermore, the business has nowhere else to go, unless they run a higher-liability discount, and then the problem starts all over again.

This problem is further compounded by having the personnel at the register ask, "Do you have any coupons today?" That customer has just been informed that somewhere out there people have coupons. Somewhere out there people are paying less for the same item than he or she has to pay. That customer may then say, "No, I don't have any coupons today. How much money did I lose?"

Then there's the chronic case of the register person who doesn't ask "Do you," but "Which coupons do you have today?" With a cross-promotion you have the ability to protect your regular price credibility. As a streetfighter, you avoid destroying your regular price credibility by transferring the responsibility of the discount to someone else.

As you'll recall from the Nautilus story, the coupons said "compliments of" the tennis club. When those 1,000 members of the tennis club received their coupons, they didn't think that the Nautilus center was providing those coupons. The "compliments of" implied that the tennis club secured those coupons for them. The members weren't given the impression that the Nautilus center was willing to discount its regular prices because they were provided to them by the tennis club. The responsibility of the discount was transferred to the tennis club.

Protecting your regular price credibility is illustrated clearly as used by a midwestern apartment complex. The city was hard hit by the automotive slow-down, and consequently most of the apartment complexes had over 20 percent vacancy. To generate leases, many of them advertised in the mass media, one month free rent with a year lease. One property was so desperate that they offered *two* months' free rent.

It was an effective offer that would be considered a high-liability discount, but it also created a problem that became an even bigger liability. The existing tenants, those 80 percent who were already residents, also wanted to take advantage of this great deal when their leases were up for renewal. If the offer was not honored, most would leave and go where it would be. If it was honored, it would cost the management thousands of dollars in lost revenue each month that the offer was in effect. In short, they destroyed their regular price credibility. They told the public and their own residents that they were desperate and were willing to make a deal to get more tenants.

Our client would have gladly given up a month's rent for a year's lease, but didn't cherish the idea of offering that same deal to the regular tenants. The solution was a cross-promotion campaign. The manager of this property approached a number of different groups,

Figure 1-7

with the biggest results from area colleges and vocational training centers where the students were in need of housing. Most schools provided the new students with packets containing brochures from the apartment complexes that would accept the students. Students were also handed a certificate from our streetfighter (Figure 1-7) that allowed one month free rent with a year's lease, compliments of that school. In all, our client was able to place about 5,000 certificates, free. More important than the free distribution was that our client was able to transfer the responsibility of the discount to the various schools. The majority of her residents had no knowledge of the special offer, and those who did knew that they didn't qualify for the special student-housing program. The free-month certificates were perceived as a benefit of being a student at that school, much like a group health plan or student aid.

In a little over four months, the apartment complex increased their occupancy from 85 to 95 percent. Not all of the increase was due to the cross-promotion, for they had a number of marketing projects going on. Yet, they didn't have to give up revenue from their regular tenants, nor did they alienate them because of the promotion.

One-Way and Two-Way—The Only Way to Fly

The stories described so far are examples of a one-way cross-promotion. This is when you have somebody else distribute your coupons for you and all you do is supply them with the coupons.

In some cases a merchant will like the idea so much that they will want you to do the same for them. This is called a two-way cross-promotion. With a two-way, you have a little more work involved in your store because you have to distribute coupons as well. However, there's nothing wrong with offering your customers a little more for their money; they'll really appreciate it.

It takes a little different approach to set the two types up. The two-way is usually easier because the merchant can readily see what is in it for them. Yet, if you set up too many two-ways, you may be spending most of your time distributing coupons at your store.

Setting Up the One-Way

Your attitude is important when approaching a potential retail partner in setting up a cross-promotion. You shouldn't think of it so much as selling, as it offers merchants an opportunity to participate in a valuable promotion. By building up the perceived value, you are most likely to get the cooperation from other merchants, not only in accepting the project, but in the proper implementation as well.

One merchant who fully understood the value of giving discount coupons to his customers saw one of his employees accidentally drop a coupon on the floor. He immediately rushed over and picked it up, telling the employee to be careful, for they were worth a lot of money. Even though they didn't cost him anything, he really felt they were of value to him and made sure his employees knew it too.

Don't be upset if you're not victorious all the time. Even the most seasoned streetfighter gets tossed out on their coupons once in a while. Stick with it. Remember, it doesn't cost a penny to ask ... the worst that could happen to you is that they say no. But keep in mind that with a fair amount of people who say yes, you'll be well on your way to increased sales.

In setting up the one-way cross-promotion follow these steps:

1. Approach the person in charge and introduce yourself. Make sure you're talking to the decision maker, not an assistant. If it's not the decision maker, don't waste your time. Find out who you need to talk to and talk to that person directly. Leaving someone to explain it secondhand hardly ever works.

2. In a low-key manner, show some samples of coupons that are similar to what you would like to do with this merchant. It's very important that you show a real live sample and not a photocopy or a rough sketch on a yellow legal pad. The live sample lends credibility to the concept. Since it was actually printed, it was obviously done elsewhere. If it's been done elsewhere, it must be legitimate. Herb Cohen, author of *You Can Negotiate Anything,* calls this "the power of legitimacy of the printed word." If you don't have samples, we'll sell you a complete packet of them. Send $5.00 and a self-addressed stamped envelope to Sample, Retail Marketing Institute, *34 W. Whittier, Columbus, OH 43206.*

3. Next, explain that you'll pay for the printing and paper for the coupons, but give him or her the credit for it. Position it as a nice surprise for their customers when they pay their bills. It's an opportunity to show appreciation to the customer for their business and it doesn't cost a thing.

4. Agree on a time span for the distribution, usually about one week. Ask for an average customer count during that time span so you know how many to print.

5. Ask for a copy of their logo, preferably black on white.

6. If you want to make the coupon compliments of the store manager, it's nice to have his or her signature (see Figure 1-8). Get it in a couple of different sizes using a black felt-tip marker. Don't use blue ink because your printer will have you shot. Blue is hard to reproduce and drives printers nuts. Using the manager's name as well as the store name is really good for getting cooperation. The manager won't want to see his or her name going to waste, and it's a nice ego trip besides. It also transfers the responsibility of the discount twice. If you really want to stroke someone, put their picture on the piece too!

7. Issue the manager a free card or token gift certificate of some kind. In the case of the Nautilus center, the manager gave the tennis club owner three free visits. He carries these cards around with him for promotional purposes. This is not a bribe, nor should it be treated as such. It's merely a thank-you for their cooperation. And their receiving something of value from you helps to ensure that your coupons will be distributed properly.

Figure 1-8

31

Figure 1-9

8. The next step is called the "glue," because it helps hold the entire promotion together. Ask the manager how many employees he or she has. Tell him or her that when you return with the coupons, you'll have something for all the employees (see Figure 1-9). It can be a 10 percent discount card or anything that is of more value than the coupons that customers will be getting, but less than the value of what the manager will receive. Let the manager know that you realize that stuffing these coupons in the bags or handing them to customers is a little extra work, so you want to provide these special coupons just for the employees. The Nautilus center used one free visit. A restaurant might use a 10 percent discount card good for 60 days.

9. Take the information to your local quick printer to get it printed. It's important that you leave yourself enough time to get it all done. Don't promise to have the coupons out in a week when you're just getting started.

Setting Up the Two-Way Cross-Promotion

1. Approach the person in charge and introduce yourself.

2. Show your samples (see Figure 1-10) and explain that it is something you saw in another area that worked pretty well.

3. Explain that with the high costs of advertising, you saw this idea and thought you'd give it a try. The idea is, that while you may have people coming to your store who have never tried their store, they may have people coming to their business who have never tried your product or

Figure 1-10

service. So the general concept is to trade customers in an attempt to generate more sales without spending a bunch of money on advertising.

4. Explain the added benefits of letting someone else assume the responsibility for the discount, and how this can help them maintain their regular price credibility.

5. Determine customer counts, agree on a time frame, offers, and expiration date. Again, be sure to give yourself plenty of time to get everything printed.

6. Generally agree to split the printing costs. It pays to have a rough estimate in various quantities.

7. Issue the free card or gift certificate and explain that you'll be bringing a little something for the employees, as explained for the one-way cross-promotion.

8. Get your logos and signatures, and head for your local quick printer.

It's important to keep in mind whenever you deal with discount coupons, that you must make sure you have all the proper disclaimers and qualifying information on it. For example, you may want to limit the coupons to one per customer. It's also a good idea to tell them that it cannot be combined with any other coupons or specials. You'll be surprised to find how many people will try to take advantage of your coupon offers. We once did a cross-over promotion with a motorcycle show where you would pay $2 for a ticket of admission but received a coupon from Pizza Hut for $2 off your next pizza. On this particular event we forgot to put "only one coupon per person, good for $2 off the regular menu price, and cannot be combined with any other special or discount."

All day we kept getting these mean-looking bikers in the store. They would order a $10 pizza, give the counter person half-a-dozen coupons, and demand $2 in change. If the biker was big enough, he got it.

Also, please don't forget an expiration date. Forgetting this type of information can cause you a lot of grief and a lot of money. Such was the case of a manager of a restaurant who read a little something about discount cards and coupons. A little information can be very dangerous! He issued 25-percent discount cards to various groups in that town, and did not put an expiration date on the card. Twenty-five percent is definitely a high liability in the restaurant business, especially when you consider that they were dealing with about 40-percent food costs. Remember, the purpose of the discount is to get people to try your place with the intention of getting them back in the future paying full price. Well, with no expiration date, these people held onto these cards forever. These weren't coupons, mind you, but discount cards that can be used over and over again. They didn't discount one item, but the entire check. People held onto these cards for years. If someone left town, they would sell it to a friend. We've even heard rumors that these cards were appearing in people's wills as part of their estates, but that was never confirmed. The point is to be careful; cover yourself. If there's a way to abuse it, someone will find it.

One at a Time/One Week at a Time

When first starting a cross-promotion program, you don't want to get overwhelmed. It can be an operational nightmare for all your employees to have to deal with too many different coupons. We generally recommend that you try to implement one cross-promotion a week, and that it last for only a week. By limiting it to a week, you usually get most of the merchant's customers one time without repeating the same people over again. Remember, you want to generate trial. If the same people receive the same coupons for weeks on end, it will lose much of the perceived value in the customer's mind, plus you stand a good chance of discounting a regular. For this reason, we usually shy away from supermarket cash-register-tape promotions. This is where they print your coupon on the back of the register tape. The negative is that they want to run these promotions for two or three months at a time. The same people would be receiving your coupons repeatedly.

There are, of course, exceptions to the one-week-at-a-time rule. For example, a restaurant set up an ongoing cross-promotion with an economy motel. The restaurant manager felt that it was a good target audience since people who were looking to save a few bucks on a motel room probably would be interested in a deal on their meal. The maids placed a discount coupon in each room daily.

The rationale was that people using motel rooms are visiting the town and not regular customers. Therefore, any business as a result of this cross-promotion involved only incremental sales.

We were also told that once in a while a regular would show up with the coupons, but the employees were instructed not to blow anyone's cover.

Your Ticket to Free Mentions

A variation on the discount-coupon program is the *ticket-to-event* cross-promotion. This particular technique was developed while consulting a Pizza Hut restaurant.

The objective was to cash in on the after-concert crowds. We waited until there was a major concert in town. When the Doobie Brothers sold out in two days, we knew that was a winner. Using a little bit of radio, we told concert-goers they could redeem their ticket stubs for a discount on their pizza after the concert. It worked. In fact, it worked too well. There was no way they could handle the tremendous volume of starving fans, most of whom were suffering from a severe case of the munchies, no doubt. The manager did what he could to keep from having a riot, which led us back to the drawing

Figure 1-11

board. We needed to see if there were any small improvements to be made, or in this case, *big* improvements.

The outgrowth of this fiasco was the ticket-to-event cross-promotion. We knew we could attract a lot of people by tying into a major event. We also know we couldn't handle the volume. We needed to find events that did not let out all at once. Consumer trade shows were the answer. We worked with the promoters of sports and vacation shows, motorcycle shows, rod and custom shows, energy shows, and so on. We provided the promoter with coupons that were equal in value to the admission price of the show, usually about $2. The promoters loved it because they could advertise a $2 admission fee, but get $2 off your next pizza (see Figure 1-11). It sounds almost like it's free.

Not only did we get all those coupons distributed at no charge, but we received mention in all the show's advertising. It was like a free mini-commercial inside a commercial.

Discount Cards, from Press to Pocketbook

We made mention of discount cards earlier, and though they may sound the same as a coupon on the surface, they're an entirely different type of promotion. There are two main differences between the discount card and the coupon: (1) The discount coupons are distributed by a merchant to customers, whereas a discount card is distributed by an organization to its members or an employer to employees (see Figure 1-12). (2) The discount card can be used over and over again for as long as the expiration date will allow; the coupon is a one-shot deal.

When dealing with discount cards, you'll find that the liability of the discount is very low. It's not so much the *amount* of the discount that makes this effective, but rather the *selectivity* of the discount. You are making their employees, students, or members feel like they are special.

PENGUIN POINT
THE PEOPLE PLEASING PLACE

DEAR EMPLOYEE:
We recently arranged with 20th Century Automotive for complimentary 10% discount cards for all our employees.

With this card you will receive a 10% discount on all labor or repair work on any vehicle you own.

This card may be used over and over again for as long as indicated by the expiration date of the card. Please note that the discount does not apply to parts or sublet work.

20th Century Automotive has the latest in computer diagnostic equipment and the most skilled automotive technicians in the area, specializing in both foreign and domestic cars.

To schedule your appointment call 432-5325.

20th **Century Automotive**
1001 Leesburg Road • Fort Wayne, Indiana
"If we can't fix it, it can't be fixed!"

DISCOUNT CARD
The bearer of this card is affiliated with

Penguin Point

and is entitled to a 10% discount on all Labor on automotive repair. Does not apply to parts.

Call for an appointment 432-5325.
Expires July 31, 1982

Figure 1-12

It's the VIP approach. When the same cards are issued with a higher-liability discount, there's no significant increase in the redemption.

The reason for the discount card as opposed to a one-time coupon is that groups seem to be willing to provide their members benefits, especially free ones. The coupon appears to be too commercial, but the discount card, like a membership card, gives them an elite status. Even though we are allowing the discount over a period of a few months, the amount of the discount is low enough so it doesn't hurt. Plus, we are protecting our regular price credibility because the organization takes full credit for the cards. When the expiration date is over, you have a good shot at keeping them as a regular customer, paying full price.

Setting up a discount card is very similar to setting up the cross-promotion. You must stress the *you* benefits. Explain that they will be able to provide their people with an extra benefit and it won't cost them a thing. Again, it's important to show the person you're dealing with an actual sample of a discount card.

You don't want to offer a discount to their people by making them show their ID at the cash register; many student discount programs are like that. In order for you to build sales from this, you must get your cards with your name on them, into the hands of all their members or employees. They need to carry it with them always. It's a constant reminder to shop at your store.

Discount cards, like coupons, are a great way of getting free distribution of your advertising. One interesting application for them was used by a carpet outlet with both retail and commercial sales. Instead of the store manager's setting up the discount-card programs with the area employers and so on, they used the discount card as an incentive for companies to buy their carpeting from this outlet. If they got the commercial order, they told the company that they would provide all company employees with discount cards for their own carpeting at no additional charge. In this manner, the store got the distribution of their discount cards as part of their regular sales program.

In the case of an independent garage, there was a mechanic who loved to talk to people. He loved to talk more than he liked fixing cars. So, for two months, they took him out from under the cars, cleaned him up, and put him on the streets setting up discount-card programs. At the same time, he was also to bring in some fleet accounts. Within two months he was responsible for distributing 20,000 discount cards, which doubled their business. It worked so well, in fact, they had to pull him off the streets and put him back under the cars. Being too successful does have its drawbacks.

Many find that large companies are more difficult to deal with, especially the personnel department. In many cases, these people have the authority to say no, but they can't say yes. If you have to wait for the committee to meet, you know you're in trouble.

We found that if you want to reach these large companies, it's generally better to work through their unions or credit unions. They really appreciate the opportunity of providing their members a benefit, especially when it doesn't cost them anything to do so. They also have a means of distribution, since they often send newsletters to their members on a monthly basis.

Beyond the Discounts

Free distribution of your advertising message doesn't always have to be limited to coupons or discount cards. Many apartment complexes like to give their residents a monthly newsletter containing information about news and policies. Our nightclub client approached a number of these apartments where they were using a plain letterhead or a hand-drawn cover. He offered to design and print the cover of their newsletter and supply them with a six-month supply of this newsletter stationery. The only thing he asked is that he get to print his ad on the back half of the page. Then the apartment would only have to type and print the inside of the newsletter and fold it. The result was that the nightclub was able to reach a large number of apartment dwellers, targeting those that were single or young couples and reminding them monthly of his place. The cost of distribution was nothing. The printing was slightly more than nothing. The results were anything but nothing.

The Essence of Streetfighting

Streetfighting is people working together to help each other get the most from their advertising budgets. It's brains over bucks, mind over money. It's creating an everyone wins situation. It's finding other businesses or organizations that stand to gain as much as you do by working together. It's the florist that teamed up with the liquor store to provide a wine-and-roses offer for Mother's Day. They shared the cost of advertising and together spent less, while making more sales than they could have separately.

Streetfighting is the little pizza stand in Lafayette, Indiana, that almost went belly-up along with his next-door neighbor, the video arcade, until they broke a hole between the two and started helping merchandise each other.

Streetfighting is the Nutri/System franchise in Charleston, West Virginia, that teamed up with a dress shop and hair salon to provide a totally "new" you.

Streetfighting is the tux shop in Los Angeles, California, that worked out cooperative programs with various high school groups around prom time to totally dominate the formal wear market for the area.

Streetfighting is boundless, limited only by your own imagination. It goes way beyond discount cards and coupons. It's getting charities to advertise for you while you help them raise money. It's getting twelve pieces of mail delivered with one stamp. It's getting free publicity. It's getting people from your front door to your cash register. It's milking the mass media for all they're worth, separating the cream from the cottage cheese, paying margarine prices but getting real butter.

2

PUBLICITY, THE FREE FORM OF ADVERTISING

Publicity is a streetfighter's dream. It offers free distribution just like a cross-promotion and has the impact of the mass media. As a matter of fact, it can create a greater impact than regular mass media advertising because it's not perceived as an ad.

When the commercials come on while you're watching TV, it's time to get another beer or relieve yourself from the last one. While driving in your car, you may find yourself pushing buttons as soon as the music ends, before you have to sit through another ration of jingles, pitches, and the ever-popular attempt at comedy. And if you had to start a cozy fire, you'd probably choose a section of the paper with a bunch of ads to get those logs started, definitely not Dear Abby, sports scores, or the Dow Jones Industrials.

With publicity you become part of the news or entertainment—the very reason people read the newspaper, watch TV, or listen to the radio. When you're interviewed on the six o'clock news, participate in a noon-time radio talk show, or have an article appear in the morning paper about your store, you're no longer advertising as far as the public is concerned. They'll therefore be more attentive to and retentive of the information.

What's News?

As with a cross-promotion, publicity can't replace your regular advertising. But it does provide a very effective supplement that will help your entire advertising program show a greater response. If you are having a clearance sale, you're not likely to get the local news media to cover it. But every time your company is mentioned in the news—whether for winning an award, helping a charitable association, or getting appointed to a cabinet position for the President of the United States—it does create awareness.

The first step is to determine what is news. There may be a lot more newsworthy items at your business than you think. If an employee gets promoted to a new position, that's news. If you are appointed to serve on a board of your trade association, that's news. Moving to a new location? That's news. Expanding an old one is news. Hiring or laying off employees is news. Introducing a new product is news. Almost everything is newsworthy provided you find the right hook or angle to capture the attention of a reporter.

Publicity is nothing new. Many fine public relations firms are paid to do nothing but keep their clients in the news. Some are paid to keep clients' names out of the news, too. Smaller businesses can't afford the services of these companies. Yet there's a lot of opportunity for you to get free publicity. Most of the "war stories" in this book were done by the merchants themselves, not by full-time PR firms. Each is an example of how a merchant was able to take advantage of a given set of circumstances to get free exposure for his or her business.

Don't Be Afraid to Ask

Reporters need you. They have deadlines. And when they have to fill space or time, they need your help most. A few may not want your help. You'll find out who they are quickly enough. Don't get discouraged, though. Most of the reporters in your community are nice people. If you have a newsworthy story, you've got a shot at getting it publicized. Always keep in mind one of the basic rules of streetfighting: Never be afraid to ask. The worst they can do is say no.

One-Trick Pony ... and No Bull

Topical items can be newsworthy, as the owner of a nightclub called Brickley's Firehouse found out. When the movie *Urban Cowboy* came out, the big craze in nightclubs was an $8000 mechanical bull.

Accompanying the craze was a lot of publicity about possible kidney damage from riding the bull. The Firehouse was a disco, not a country music club, but in this particular market all the clubs were competing for business. To capture some of that country crowd, a Tuesday promotion called "Bourbon Cowboy Night" was started.

There were rumors around town that one of the country music clubs had a bull on order. Obviously, the first club in town to get one would get a great deal of news coverage, not to mention all the bar business for a time.

To make use of the excitement about the first bull in town, a press release was sent out to all the news media announcing the grand unveiling of The Firehouse Mechanical Horse. It was very carefully worded to say that the mechanical horse was not to be confused with the mechanical bull. The horse was specifically designed for the purpose of amusement, whereas the bull's primary function was to train rodeo participants. Furthermore, to the best of their knowledge, there had never been an injury in any nightclub throughout the country on this particular model.

Since it was the first such riding device to hit the bars in this area, it captured a tremendous amount of coverage. The local country radio station even cosponsored the event, including one live announcement every hour for five days, free. They even provided one of their jocks to serve as the "Bat Masterson of Ceremonies."

Then at precisely 10:00 P.M., to the tune of "Back in the Saddle Again," the canvas was lifted to reveal the first mechanical horse.

Silence.

Then a sudden burst of laughter filled the room as the crowd realized that the mechanical horse was just that—a riding horse. The same kind of riding horse that a two-year-old begs his parents to put a quarter in so he can play Roy Rogers.

The DJ was the first to take a ride, and since DJs are supposed to be entertaining, he demonstrated some pretty fancy riding stunts: Fancy mounts and dismounts. Standing, side saddle, and one very interesting maneuver that looked as if he'd graduated from the Dudley Doright School of Mechanical Horse Riding.

At any rate, everyone had a great time and it was a fantastic idea. Well, almost everybody. There was one real cowboy who drove 400 miles to practice for a rodeo. It took close to a case of Jack Daniels to calm him down. He eventually put his six-shooter away and slowly drove his pickup into the sunrise.

Some interesting side notes. First, instead of having to spend $8000 on a bull they didn't want, they were able to pick up this soon-to-be-antique for a mere 50 bucks. Not only that; similar devices found in front of K-Mart stores charge a quarter, while this one cost only a dime. This was truly the "savings place."

Even more interesting: When the competitor finally did get the mechanical bull, the local paper did a full-page spread on it as predicted. But almost half of the article was devoted to the mechanical horse! So not only were they able to capture the excitement of a very topical item, but they were also able to take a little steam away from the competition.

A couple of questions usually come up whenever we tell this story. First, was the media upset because there was no real mechanical bull? In this case, no. But sometimes you'll run into a reporter without a sense of humor. You have to look at the possible downsides of any promotion you do. They were questioned about it, though. The manager merely showed them a copy of the release and reiterated that they went to great pains in the release to avoid confusion.

The second question is, was there a fear that the stunt would have back-fired on them, with the crowd enacting a modern version of the OK Corral? There was that concern, but they were reasonably confident of their crowd. They knew their customers and felt secure with the promotion.

Who to Woo

Each newsworthy item doesn't appeal to every newsperson. The trick is matching up the news item to the reporter or reporters who are most likely to do the story. This is really to your advantage because you don't want to constantly contact the same reporter week in and week out. Too much may cause contempt. Therefore, spread your wealth of information. That's why it's so important to find that "hook" or "angle."

Each news medium, but especially daily newspapers, have certain reporters that cover a specific area. One editor for sports, and another for business or finance. You'll probably find a family editor, religious editor, entertainment editor, and so on. If a particular item fits better in a certain section of the paper, that should be the reporter you contact. Or, by taking what might be a general news item and giving it a little twist to appeal to a specific editor, you have greater flexibility in the people you can contact.

Putting Some Punch in Their Publicity

One of the more well-rounded publicity campaigns was done by the Parker Shelton School of Karate. Though it was a business, it was run like a club, with each student having specific responsibilities. One student was appointed Publicity Chairperson. His primary function was to inform the sports editors of all the local newspapers, radio, and TV stations when one of the students won a trophy in competition. They were very active in sport karate, and there would usually be a group traveling out of town on the weekend to participate in a tournament. Often, they would come back with a couple of awards in a number of divisions.

The local press was pretty good about reporting on their victories. There would usually be a small paragraph in both dailies, and at least one of the TV stations and a couple of the radio stations would mention it if time permitted.

This obviously helped keep the name of the Parker Shelton School of Karate in the public's mind. Not only that, but since the news item was about winners, it also conveyed an image of a very credible and effective school, with quality instruction.

There was another plus as well. Students who heard their names on the air or saw them in the paper really got fired up and worked harder to win more tournaments—which resulted in more publicity. And the more publicity a student got, the more friends would start asking about taking karate lessons, resulting in new dues-paying students for the school.

The publicity chairperson, though only a blue belt in rank (intermediate level), turned out to be a black belt in public relations. He got a tremendous amount of coverage with the sports editors. But competition was just one of many aspects of this martial art. He started working on other hooks (and we don't mean punches).

He called the women's editor at one of the papers and talked to her about self-defense for women. He told her that the school had some female instructors and that they taught a special class in women's self-defense. He felt that her readers would be very interested in an article on the class. She agreed, and a full-page article, complete with photographs, was the result.

A little more confident now, he called the producer of the local noon TV talk shows. One item mentioned was how many young children were enrolled in karate classes by their parents to help teach them discipline. Some students were as young as seven. Teaching young children discipline was the "hook." The young students, accompanied by their parents and the instructor, made for a very interesting 30-minute interview.

After that, he approached a business reporter for the number-one-rated radio station and told him about some of the area executives and business people who took karate as a means of helping them deal with stress. This same angle was later used on another noon TV talk show.

Many times the school would get a student with a handicap. Karate was then used as a form of therapy, and Parker Shelton was very good with these people. Most would never become extremely proficient. But they would gain a great deal of improvement in mobility and self-esteem. Polio victims, amputees, and even a blind student caught the interest of the local media. In these situations, the city desk editor was contacted since it would be considered more of a general news item.

After getting a reporter interested in a particular item about the karate school, the publicity person would often, as the clincher, offer an exclusive. That meant that none of that reporter's competition would be contacted about the story. (Competition meaning someone within the same medium.) If an exclusive was promised to a newspaper, no other paper would get it. But a radio or TV station could.

Another area for gaining publicity is public appearances. There are many clubs and organizations always looking for a thirty-minute program, and the karate school would be ready to demonstrate. When such a demonstration was lined up, a press release was sent out that many times received a little air play from the broadcasters and a blurb in the paper.

One public appearance resulted in statewide TV coverage. Part of karate training revolves around the practice of "kata." (Literally translated, it means "form.") This is where the student performs a prearranged series of fighting movements that represent defending against a number of imaginary opponents. It looks similar to a floor exercise in gymnastics only with blocks, punches, kicks, and a loud "kiai" or scream. Four of the advanced students put together a special kata that they performed in unison to the "William Tell Overture" (more commonly known as the theme from "The Lone Ranger"). Needless to say, they were moving very rapidly.

After seeing this demonstration and the tremendous crowds reaction to it, Indiana University officials invited them to perform in Bloomington during halftime at the IU vs. Illinois basketball game. Not only were there an estimated 17,000 people in the audience, but the demonstration was televised throughout the entire state. It sure made a big impact back home. (IU won the game by the way. Coach Bobby Knight holds a black belt in basketball.)

Almost any merchant can do exactly what this karate student did. Obviously, some types of businesses lend themselves more to publicity than others. Yet, coming up with that hook can help you cash in on some of this free exposure.

Rounding Up a Reporter Roster

Before you can begin your publicity campaign, you must first determine all the available sources for getting your publicity out to the public. Make a list of all the print media in your area. That includes daily newspapers, weeklies, tabloids, cable TV magazines, city magazines, entertainment magazines, and local business journals. Don't forget the suburban papers or papers from small towns in the area. Then, to that list add all the TV and radio stations in the area. You can even include PBS and religious stations. You might even consider some large company's internal newsletter, or maybe even some church bulletins or neighborhood newsletters. Look for anything that might get you exposure, free.

When mailing to this list, you'll need their mailing address and phone number. It's best to have the name of the person whom you want to read the release. A daily newspaper may have a dozen or more listings because of the specialization of each editor.

To save time when sending out information, it would help to have this list typed on a mailing list label sheet. This grid sheet allows you to put 33 labels on a single page and can be photocopied directly onto pressure-sensitive self-adhesive mailing labels. It sure beats typing or hand addressing the envelopes every time you want to send out a release. Also, run a copy of the master list on a regular sheet of paper so you can add the phone number of each contact.

When you need to change a label on your master sheet, just type the new name and address on a blank label then stick it over the old one. You should try to update your list at least every six months.

You'll probably be able to find most of the media listed in the phone book. For broadcast, look in the white pages under *W,* since they are listed by their call letters. (In western states, look under *K;* Canadian stations should be listed under *C.*) They also might be listed in the Yellow Pages under broadcast stations or advertising.

Print media are often found under *Newspaper* in the Yellow Pages. You can also check the *Standard Rate and Data Service* (SRDS) in the local library. There should be one for radio, TV, newspapers, and magazines. Also, in most public libraries, you'll find the *Ayer Directory* and *Bacon's Publicity Checker.*

Write 'Em or Ring 'Em?

With this newly compiled information, you still have two different ways of contacting the media. You can send them a press release or give them a call. And sometimes you might want to do both.

If you have a relatively simple news item with plenty of lead time, a press release may be all you need. This works particularly well on news items announcing an upcoming event. On the other hand, if you want to get publicity on an event that just took place, you'd better get on the phone. Reporters don't like to report yesterday's news.

When trying to secure a feature story, it could go either way depending on the preference of the reporter. Most merchants don't have the time to sit down and write a formal press release, print it, and mail it. However, 20 minutes on the phone after lunch can be worked in nicely. You have to play it by ear in many cases. Try to develop a system that works for you. If you can dictate a release in a couple of minutes and have your secretary handle it from there, great. But, if you don't have dictation equipment, or at least a secretary, let your fingers do the talking.

Burger Boo Boo Gets Last Laugh

Here is a wonderful story of how a few phone calls and some fast thinking ended up with a lot of publicity. It happened at a Burger Chef Restaurant in Indianapolis (since bought out by Hardee's). They were just introducing their new drive-thru window service. At one of the stores, on the first day, the first person drove up and gave the first order. Everything worked wonderfully. It was first-rate all the way. The second person drove up and wanted to make a bank deposit!

The manager thought this was funny. He told the story to his supervisor, who thought it was funny. The supervisor told the account executive the story, and he laughed because the client was laughing. The account executive wrote a brief note to the Public Relations Department telling of the event and requested a little action. The note was received by a very young, creative, streetfighting type who was destined to coauthor a book someday about his unusual advertising techniques. He laughed a lot. He then got on the phone and called the item in to one of the newspapers, and the city desk editor started laughing. He then called the other major newspaper (since he didn't promise an exclusive) and that editor started laughing as well. This got the young PR man very excited. He then called one of the top-rated radio stations in the city and told the story to the afternoon jock, who broke out laughing. Next he called all the local TV stations and told the story to each anchor person, and every time they laughed.

The punch line for a half hour of phone calling was a paragraph on the front page of the *Indianapolis News* and a story in the Sunday edition of the *Star.* The jock on WIBC told the story on the air to the traffic reporter in the helicopter—the primest of prime time in radio. Also, it was the ending story on the ABC affiliate's late news. So excited was he that he even sent a telegram to the "Tonight Show." Unfortunately, Johnny Carson didn't laugh.

In this case, had he sent a press release, it wouldn't have had the response that it did. And with that response they were able to gain a lot of exposure for their new drive-up window that would have cost them tens of thousands of dollars to achieve otherwise . . . and that's no laughing matter.

Rewarding Rewards Very Rewarding

Here's another example of how the phone was used to create an exceptional amount of publicity from all the news media. In this case, however, only one phone call was made!

A tavern hired a couple of off-duty police officers to check IDs at the front door and patrol the parking lot on busier nights. One of these officers was severely beaten while patronizing another bar. The TV stations covered the story immediately and interviewed him from his hospital bed when he could barely talk. All the news media carried the event. Many times it was the lead story, and the entire community was shocked by this event.

The owner of the tavern where this policeman worked part-time called the mayor's office and offered a $1000 reward for any information leading to the arrest and conviction of the persons responsible for the beating. The mayor's office jumped right on it and set a meeting with the police department public relations officer. He, in turn, set up a press conference to announce the reward.

The next day the story of the reward was carried on all the TV and radio stations along with all newspapers in the area. The amount of the time and space that was used would have cost three to four times the reward, maybe more.

The next day the owner of the bar where the beating took place offered to underwrite half of the reward. This reduced the iiability of the first tavern to $500 and another round of publicity started because of this twist.

They never had to pay the reward money (which they would have gladly done), for the culprits were never caught. But regardless, the goodwill and exposure created from this gesture were priceless.

Forget-Me-Not with TV Publicity

One phone call from Doug Hackbarth of Broadview Florists resulted in a publicity series that lasted longer than many new prime-time TV shows. After attending one of our seminars, Doug simply called up a reporter at the number-one-rated TV news team in town and suggested that viewers would be very interested in a week-long series on the care and feeding of household flowers and plants.

The reporter thought a week-long series was out of the question, but a weekly series would be fine. So, every Tuesday on the noon, early, and late news, there was a minute-and-a-half segment on plants, featuring Doug.

It ran for a total of seventeen months! He's become somewhat of a local celebrity to flower enthusiasts in his area. And anyone who walks into his shop immediately recognizes him as the number-one expert. They buy whatever he recommends.

If he had to pay for the exposure on that station, it would have cost him well over $50,000. But, he got it free. Of course, it wasn't a real commercial since he couldn't directly advertise his business. Yet the obvious conclusion would have been to follow the free publicity with a TV and newspaper campaign featuring Doug as the expert.

There is also a "snowball" effect when you start getting publicity on this level. Doug has since been in the paper, on radio shows, and most recently on a four-part series on another television station. Whenever there's a florist- or greenhouse-related story for which reporters need a local authority, Doug is the first one they think of.

Put It in Writing with a Press Release

If you have plenty of time, a press release may be the way to go. It could save you a lot of time on the phone on those simple news items, such as announcing an employee's promotion, that need to go to a few dozen reporters. The press release tells the story you want the reporter to cover, but you must provide it in an acceptable format for the best results (see example, Figure 2-1).

The first part of the release tells the reporter whom to contact if more information is needed. Put "For Further Information Contact:" on the top of the page. This is followed by the name of the contact, mailing address, and phone number. Skip a few spaces and put "Release Date: Immediate." Skip a few more spaces, center, put the headline. They probably won't use your headline, but at least it will give the reporter a good idea about the content.

Now you're ready to write the body of the release. The first paragraph should answer the questions who, what, why, where, when, and how. The rest of the release deals with the details.

Retail Marketing Institute
34 W. Whittier Street   Columbus, Ohio 43206
614/443-5555

FOR IMMEDIATE RELEASE

For further info contact:

Marc Slutsky
Vice President
Retail Marketing Institute
34 W. Whittier Street
Columbus, OH 43205
614/443-5555

Streetfighting Marketing Seminar Offered In Columbus

COLUMBUS, OH -- The Retail Marketing Institute, a Columbus based marketing company, announced that September 30 is the date of the first public "Streetfighting Marketing" seminar to be offered this year. The "Streetfighting" seminar is a half-day program that teaches businesses how to advertise, promote, and market their products and services on a shoe-string budget.

This public seminar is geared for the individual business unit that either can't afford to spend money for advertising, or wants to supplement their regular advertising budget with inexpensive techniques.

The Streetfighting concept was developed by the company's founder and President, Jeff Slutsky, who will conduct the program on September 30, at the Radisson Hotel beginning at 6:30 p.m.. This program is noted nationally for its hard hitting "how-to" content presented in an entertaining and lively manner. The tuition is $305 per person with discounts available for groups and non-profit organizations.

Slutsky is the author of the Prentice-Hall book, <u>Streetfighting: Low Cost Advertising/Promotion For Your Small Business</u>, which is ready to go into its second printing.

The "Streetfighting" client list is an impressive collection of major organizations which have included Walgreens, Amoco Oil, McDonald's, Arby's, American Express, National Car Rental, Weight Watchers, Viking/White Sewing Machine Company, and The Government Of India. This is the company's eighth year of operation. They relocated to Columbus from Chicago just under three years ago, and also operates a second office in Dallas, Texas.

Interested business people can get additional information about the seminar by contacting the Retail Marketing Institute at 443-5555.

#######

Figure 2-1

52

Many reporters are very sensitive to news items that appear to be "too commercial." If it looks as if the only reason for the item is to plug the name of your company, there's a good chance it won't be used. A more subtle approach may yield better results.

The Bare Facts

A press release was used by a Naked Furniture franchisee to get some exposure for an upcoming promotion. As the name of the store suggests, they sell unfinished furniture. But the store name raised some eyebrows in this particularly conservative community.

The biggest problem, though, was that the store was located on one of the busiest intersections in the city, yet very few people seemed to notice it. Something needed to be done to get the attention of passing motorists to fully take advantage of this high visibility location.

As it turned out, a campaign was launched by the Citizens for Decency to rid their fair community of all the dirty bookstores and X-rated movie theaters. Pickets worked around the clock discouraging would-be consumers from partaking of this illicit entertainment.

It's just the type of news item the media loves, and they covered it very emphatically. Soon, the entire city was aware of the picketing. According to one of the bookstore owners, the publicity actually doubled their business. And if the picketers didn't come back next month, they'd have to go out and hire some.

Whether that was true or not, we don't know. But, it did spark an idea for the owner of the Naked Furniture store. He hired picketers—theater students from a local junior college—to picket his store on a Saturday afternoon.

The theme of the picketers was "Naked People . . . No! Furniture . . . Yes!" About a week prior to the scheduled picketing, a press release was sent out announcing this event. The hook was that the owner was demonstrating his sympathy for the Citizens for Decency and their wish to clean up the city. He also wanted to clear up any confusion there might be about the name of his franchise.

The primary reason for the picketing was to draw attention to the store from passing cars. Yet by using a program that tied in with a current event and a press release, they were able to get the media interested in it as well.

The Promotion Promotion

As was stated before, when an employee is hired and/or promoted within your organization you usually have a number of outlets for getting publicity. This type of item almost always requires a release because the reporters want the information in writing. It won't be a feature story, but it often gets a mention during the business report or in the business section of the paper.

When a new DJ of a popular nightclub was first hired, a brief press release was sent out to announce it. In this particular market, two TV stations had a special portion of their Sunday evening newscast devoted to just such events. One of the leading radio stations reported these items every day during afternoon drive time. Both dailies would usually give it a blurb, and the local tabloid would print the release in its entirety, usually with a photograph. Once in a while some of the other broadcast stations would pick it up too, if it was a slow news day.

Those little news items brought such a response that they decided to promote the DJ to a new position the following month. He became the Creative Director. His salary didn't change, nor did his responsibilities. The only thing that changed was his title. A press release went out and once again it was mentioned by two TV stations, one radio station, both newspapers, and the tabloid.

The Creative Director thought this was great. He just loved getting all this attention. So, about a month or so later, he was promoted to the position of Entertainment Coordinator. His friends called to congratulate him. His mother was very proud of him. He got at least three short notes from life insurance sales reps, and of course, the name of the business received a little more free exposure.

The Entertainment Coordinator, now very excited, was promoted six weeks later to the newly created position of Director of Consumer Affairs. Since there were quite a few affairs going on at this place, it was a highly regarded position. It was also a highly publicized position, getting exposure on TV, radio, and in print once again.

It must have been very obvious to the management that this employee was really going places. It couldn't have been more than two months later when the Director of Consumer Affairs took over his new position as Vice President of Customer Relations. Not only did they get the publicity again, but one area bank even sent him a nice potted plant for his new office. Unfortunately, there wasn't much room for it with all the record albums and electronic equipment crammed in his little booth.

It wasn't until he was promoted from Vice President of Customer Relations to the new position of DJ that the media finally caught on. So now, instead of promoting him, they just change his name every few months.

Creating News When There Is None

Oftentimes you may find yourself with nothing newsworthy to give to the media. That's when you have to create an event so you have something to report. The promotion promotion might be considered a publicity stunt because the only reason they went to the trouble was for the free exposure. On the other hand, the picketing program in front of the Naked Furniture store would have been done anyway. In that case the publicity was just icing on the cake—or perhaps the varnish on the chair.

The publicity stunt should be a carefully organized event, which means you'll have plenty of time to send out a release and follow up with a phone call. You're also looking to get a feature story as opposed to a blurb.

One good way to get the media interested is to plan something really big ... or really small. It can be the highest or the shortest, the heaviest or the lightest, the prettiest or the ugliest. Look in the *Guiness Book of World Records* for starters. If your maintainance man doesn't resemble the Elephant Man, you'll have to resort to making or doing something novel.

The World's Longest Pizza

A very elaborate publicity stunt was done by a Pizza Hut franchisee in Bluffton, Indiana. As part of an annual parade and festival, this Pizza Hut was going to bake the world's longest pizza.

A special oven had to be brought in to bake this monstrosity, and when they were first testing the oven a week before the big event, a press release was sent out. Not much was expected for the test, but oddly enough, a couple of TV stations showed up with mini-cams to cover it. You never know what the media want. A week later the event received tremendous coverage once again. The pizza turned out to be 160 feet long, and the entire thing was marched in the parade by 45 volunteers.

When in Doubt, Feed Them

One other approach to getting the participation of the media for what might be considered an otherwise uneventful story is to feed them. A supermarket chain was holding a press conference to announce something or other. The press release was followed up with a phone call to a local TV station inviting the press to a luncheon press conference. The reporter covered up the receiver with his hand and yelled to the camerman, "Hey Mac! Are you up for a free meal at the country club today?"

Do It by Request

Radio stations can offer many opportunities for publicity. A Nautilus Fitness Center wanted to get its name mentioned on the station it played during workouts. So one of the instructors called the station on the request hot line, and in her sexiest voice requested the song "Physical" by Olivia Newton-John. Not only was it high on the song charts then, but it tied in well with the club.

She also told the jock that she had been working very hard trying to develop her "pecs" which is short for pectoral, the muscles that form the chest. Obviously, that's all the DJ needed once he got back on the air. With a line like that he just couldn't leave it alone, telling his audience about the caller from the Nautilus club who was working on her pecs. He then made a comment on how he wouldn't mind helping her exercise, and then he played the request.

Fortunately this was radio and the jock couldn't see the instructor, who stood about six-one, weighed 180 pounds, and could bench press a Mack truck with full saddle tanks.

The owner of a printing shop in Baltimore, Maryland, was also able to get some free exposure from the radio stations. As soon as the station started announcing all the school and business closings due to weather, he would call in that all three shifts should report on time.

All three shifts consisted of his wife working the front counter and himself in the back running the press.

Trade-Offs in Trade Mags

Many merchants, once they start getting some publicity in the market, like to see their names in the trade journals as well. If you win an award of some kind or get appointed to a board position, there's no problem. As a matter of fact, you can use that for local publicity too. But be very careful of the type of interview you give to a trade journal.

Your customers read the daily newspaper, not your trade journal. So, other than massaging your ego, it has no real advantage. It can even be a real disadvantage. A carpet-cleaning operation had a great article written about how it was blowing the door off in its Florida location. The feature really was a great stroke. So impressive, in fact, that a number of carpet-cleaning operaters decided to move there. Now sales aren't as good.

Most News Is Good News

There always is the question of bad publicity. Yes, there are times when a certain news item can really hurt business. But before you kill a news item, make sure it really is negative.

A bar was being challenged by the Neighborhood Association on its liquor license renewal. The residents were complaining about too much noise, beer cans everywhere, and even patrons urinating in the streets. A local reporter jumped right on the controversy, and the owner was really worried that it might be bad for business.

As it turned out, it was one of the best things that ever happened to his business. Most of the patrons were young, single, beer-guzzling rowdies. They could not have cared less about the neighborhood. As far as readers like them were concerned, it sounded as if everyone was having a great time, so business picked up.

As soon as the owner realized that it was actually good for business, he dragged out the renewal process for as long as possible, making sure to leak the items to the press every step of the way.

This same owner got a great idea for a promotion out of an article in *The Wall Street Journal*. He started taping "General Hospital" every day on his home video recorder. Then on Saturday afternoons, he would play all five hours of that week's episodes on his big-screen TV. This was a dead time for his place normally. But after a month it started to pick up. Mostly working women came in. Drinks were two-for-one, and the word got out fast. Soon the men got wind of it and they started showing up too. Not necessarily to watch the soap, but to watch the women watch the soap. After all, here were these women watching people on the screen doing what the men were thinking, and the entire time guzzling down strawberry daquiris as if there was no tomorrow.

It so happens there was no tomorrow. It wasn't long thereafter when one of the newspapers found out and did close to a full-page article about the promotion. That was great for business. But then ABC in New York received a copy of the article and sent a telegram to the owner telling him to cease and desist or get sued.

After consulting a copyright attorney, he decided to honor ABC's wishes. But he also contacted the same reporter who did the original story and told her what had happened. She printed another story about ABC's demand. It was very good publicity for the bar, but not so good for ABC.

Our Point of View on Interviews

With features like consumer hotlines or trouble shooter, you may find yourself face-to-face someday with a reporter complete with a video camera, large wooden cross, and three nails.

Before agreeing to any interview, try to get as much information from the reporter as possible. Even so, once those lights go on they may try to give you a hard way to go. So take the time before the interview to think of every possible question that can be asked. Then think of a response for each question. And then, practice! Get yourself a couple of journalism majors from a local junior college and pay them to drill you. If you can find one that idolizes Mike Wallace, all the better. Then practice being calm and saying exactly what you want to say.

Don't say anything off the record. Ever! There's no such thing as off the record.

If you don't quite understand the question or need more time to answer, ask the reporter to rephrase the question. Also, repeating the question helps buy some time. For example, you can answer a question with, "As I understand it, you want to know if. . . ."

Don't lose your temper. You'll really come off looking bad if you do. If you don't know the answer to a question, don't be afraid to say you don't know. But offer to find it out if they like.

Lastly, be very careful with your wording. Skillful editors can clip and splice so that what you say on the air and what you said during the interview have completely different meanings.

It would help before being interviewed by a given reporter to see or read some of their other stories. This will give you a decent idea of how they might cover you.

The word is: Be prepared.

We Practice What We Preach

One final note: When we were first approached by *INC. Magazine* to do a feature on streetfighting (the result of a simple release), we knew it was our first shot at some national publicity. When they got to the part where they hired a photographer to take pictures for the article, the reporter wanted to get a shot of us consulting a client. That was no problem.

But, if we could somehow get a picture of our newsletter, *Streetfighter,* in the picture, it would do us more good as far as our bottom line is concerned. We suggested that an interesting picture would be a shot of both of us in front of this large mural of the cover of one of the issues of *Streetfighter.* The reporter loved the idea.

We had just 48 hours to get such a mural made before the photographer showed up.

Being the streetfighers that we are . . . we did.

3

COMMUNITY INVOLVEMENT AND YOUR BOTTOM LINE

For most, *community involvement* somehow brings forth images of old money—rich widowers doling out fistfuls of dollars to civic foundations; appointments to strings of honorary board chairmanships; and other time-consuming projects. Streetfighters know better!

Streetfighters know when to say yes and how to say no to public-service requests. And how to get it accomplished in the least amount of time. They seem to give away thousands of dollars a year . . . but do they really? They learn to spot an opening for a little extra twist here and there that can turn an out-and-out donation into a successful promotional community-service tie-in.

The Low-Liability/High-Visibility Strategy

The low-liability/high-visibility strategy comes into play after you've made the decision to work with an organization. Now the key is to look for ways of getting the maximum exposure for the least investment in both time and money.

Most businesses are besieged by countless requests from nonprofit organizations for donations. Many of these may provide you with opportunities to get very positive exposure in your community. But you need to develop a system that is based on product-cost dollars or percentage of sales, so that your donation is somehow tied to a purchase. This keeps your investment in money to a minimum.

You also need to develop a system that allows the group,

suppliers, or some other outside source to handle most of the coordination of your participation in the program. This keeps your investment in time to a minimum.

When an organization asks you for help, ask yourself these questions: Will the group promote my company? Can it get me publicity? Can the promotion be tied to sales? But before any such groups will be willing to provide you with this kind of exposure, you'll have to provide them with something of value, too. In many situations all you need to provide is a vehicle by which they can raise the money they need. In other words, you have to create the "everyone-wins" situation. This is vital to streetsmart community-involvement programs and every single aspect of streetfighting.

Are You Advertising, or Giving Money Away?

It's important for you to know the difference. If you have money and choose to give it away to a worthy cause, that's your business. There are hundreds of worthy charities and community projects that can use your dollars, and it's not the purpose here to discourage you from giving money away. Donate your last dollar. Tithe to your heart's content, if that's what you want to do. But don't make the mistake of giving money away and calling it advertising!

Perhaps the most classic example of this is *program advertising.* There are high school plays, sporting events, yearbooks, and dozens of variations that you as a retailer are called upon to buy every year. In most cases, you are giving money away.

Ask yourself this question: At the last event I attended at which I received a program, did I read it? Did I take it home with me? Do I remember any of the ads contained in the program, with the possible exception of mine or my competitors? And most important, did I spend a single dollar as a result of any ad in that program?

Granted, there are exceptions. And there are times when you feel you absolutely have to buy the lousy ad—such as when one of your best customer's kids ask you. So take out the smallest ad they have to offer. You're still not advertising. It's a donation, pure and simple.

Another exception might be a speed shop in a stock-car-racing program, a piano dealer at a recital, or possibly a dance studio at a ballet program. But these are products that are tied to the event in question and even then, you should watch out for what's called the "cancel-out effect."

If every speed shop in the city is also in that racing program, does anyone really benefit? Streetfighters in this case aren't afraid to ask for exclusivity so that they will be the only speed shop in the program. They might not get it, but it doesn't cost a penny to ask.

Runaway Sales with a Throwaway Ad

There are times when you can turn a "throwaway" ad into a good promotional program. A good example of this was the restaurant manager who was approached to buy an ad in a dance recital program for $15. Before turning the request down (which is an art in itself, as you will learn a little later in this chapter), he took a moment to ask a couple of questions. It turned out that the event was being held just three blocks from his location on a Monday night the following month. He also discovered that the program was being sold for fifty cents and that last year the event drew about 300 people.

The wheels started grinding in his head. He probed further. He found out that the recital started at six o'clock and let out at eight o'clock. Hmmm ... he tried to envision himself as one of the proud parents of a miniature Baryshnikov. He imagined his son, the star defensive tackle for his junior high school, getting ready for the dance recital. Since it takes close to an hour to don full gridiron battle gear, it would take at least half that time to put on a set of tights, tutu, and toe shoes. That includes time for some last-minute alterations by Mommy. So if the show starts at six o'clock, that means that Bruiser will have to be there, all decked out, by no later than five-thirty. That also means that these people probably won't have a chance to eat dinner before the recital.

Even the average retailer might have figured this one out, had he or she taken the time to ask some questions. But, the average retailer would have probably put a coupon in the program.

Not this guy, he's a streetfighter par excellence; and rather than keep you in suspense any longer, here's what he did: First he bought the fifteen-dollar throwaway ad, then he asked the student salesman if he thought he could sell more programs at the event if he gave the buyers a dollar back with every purchase.

The student looked at him rather strangely. While it certainly would increase sales, he didn't quite understand the mathematics.

Our streetfigher then went to the cash register and pulled out what looked like a dollar bill (see Figures 3-1 and 3-2) and handed it to the young man. "This is our Dinner Dollar coupon. It's good for a dollar off the regular price of any of our complete dinners. And since we like to help out anything that has to do with kids, we'll give you $300 worth of these so you can stick them inside the programs. We'll make these coupons compliments of your group, and we'll even pick

Figure 3-1

Figure 3-2

up the cost of the printing." WOW! The young salesperson had never heard of such a deal. This guy had a heart of gold!

Not really. He's a streetfighter and a very good one at that. Examine the thought process that went into this transaction. Monday is without question the worst night of the week in almost any restaurant in the country. The thought of 300 potential customers right in his back yard on a Monday night got his attention right away.

But why the hassle of printing the extra coupons? Why not use the ad and get your coupon out that way? Remember, program ads very seldom get read, much less acted upon. By getting distribution of the coupon, which incidentally was a different color paper, he was able to dominate the book. It was the first thing people saw. Since it was loose in the book, half of them probably fell out on the floor. Since they looked a little like a dollar bill, many people would pick them up.

Also, note the way the streetfighter carefully constructed the everyone-wins situation, how he said $300 worth of coupons, not 300 coupons. Did he give away $300? Certainly not. But the junior sales rep thought so.

Even if every coupon got redeemed, the streetfighter was giving away *product-cost dollars* as opposed to real dollars. Probably 35 to 45 percent in the restaurant business. Keep in mind that in order to get those dollars, people had to purchase a meal.

The bottom line of the promotion, in addition to the community involvement benefits: business tripled that Monday night. Plus, many of those people were first-time patrons with the potential of becoming regulars. Not a bad night's work for a $15 ad, $10 worth of printing, and a fair amount of streetsmart thinking.

This story may be somewhat reminiscent of cross-promotions and discount cards, and in many ways it is. But there are some differences that make the community involvement variation very special. First of all, one of the major differences is in the method of distribution. In a cross-promotion the coupons are distributed by another merchant as an added value to his or her customers. With a discount card, the distribution is usually provided by associations, schools, groups, or companies as an added benefit for their members, students, or employees. The community involvement version gets distribution by nonprofit organizations to members of the community. It's provided as an aid to help these groups sell whatever it is they are selling—

whether it's raffle tickets, candy, cookies, magazines, even program ads. And it's using product-cost dollars!

Product-Cost Dollars vs. Real Dollars

When you buy an ad in the mass media, they send you a bill. When you pay that bill, unless you've set up a trade, it will be with *real dollars.* The exciting aspect of community involvement is that you're dealing with *product-cost dollars.* You may be providing hundreds of dollars worth of help to charitable groups, but what's the real, bottom-line cost to you? It's what *you* paid for that product or service. The higher the profit margin you work with, the more attractive working with product-cost dollars can be.

Another aspect of many of the community involvement programs using product-cost dollars is that it requires a purchase to take advantage of the offer. In that regard it's very much like having a coupon redeemed.

Even when a donation is asked for, giving away product-cost dollars is to your advantage. A $100 donation costs you $100 whereas donating a $100 piece of merchandise for a charity auction or raffle may cost you only $50. It also gives you the opportunity to unload a slow mover while getting some mileage out of it. Plus, the publicity you get from the promotion as a result of your donation will be centered around a specific product that allows for greater identification of your store.

Witches, Woofers, Speakers, and Spooks

One of the better examples of using product-cost dollars for a community involvement program had to be when a stereo dealer *loaned* about $3,000 worth of sound equipment to a fund-raising haunted house.

As the result of their participation in the program, they became a cosponsor of the event, just for lending the equipment. The store became a distribution point for tickets, there were free mentions on the radio, and their logo was on all the posters.

It was definitely high visibility. And the cost? Zero. As a matter of fact, the promotion gave the stereo dealer a perfectly legitimate reason to have a sale with all this very slightly used equipment!

The Low-Liability Device

One method of utilizing high visibility/low liability is by developing a special coupon just like the dinner dollar to be used exclusively for charity groups. Avoiding its use with merchants for cross-promotions helps to protect the credibility and believability of the special coupon. This coupon is what is called a low-liability discount, one with a slight discount. Generally, redemption is not the main objective as much as the overall visibility in the community. What usually happens is that after people receive this special coupon, they'll often receive another coupon with a larger discount or higher liability from a cross-promotion.

The reason you should want to consider a low-liability discount for your public-service coupon is that it's an ongoing program. If you use a high-liability (deeper) discount, there might be peak seasons when you don't want to nor have the need to discount as deeply. Then when the nonprofit organization needs dinner dollars, beef bucks, clean-car cash, matzoh money, or whatever you decide to call it, you don't turn them down. For if you do, and they feel that the only reason for supplying them with these coupons is to increase your business, the entire program will lose its credibility. This should be a program that is set up for the specific purpose of helping the various community organizations.

Here's how the device works. When a nonprofit organization is selling raffle tickets, candy, or whatever, door-to-door, the first question people ask is, "How much?" The kids then reply that the ticket cost $1 but with each one you buy, you get a dollar off your next meal at Jeff & Woody's Prime Rib.

This gives the illusion that the raffle ticket is free, which makes these programs easier to sell. Whether or not it really does is immaterial. The point is that the kids think it helps, and that alone may give them greater confidence, thus improving their sales. It also provides instant gratification. The buyer may not win the raffle but still gets an immediate value for the donation.

There's another advantage to this program. You're getting a five-second live commercial door-to-door provided by the nonprofit organization in your city. Your business is associated with helping worthwhile organizations, your name is mentioned, your coupons are distributed, yet your contribution in both time and money is kept to a minimum, low liability.

To speed up the process, a simple mailing to nonprofit organizations in your area will help to get the word out (see Figures 3-3, 3-4, 3-5, and 3-6). You can get the list either free or for a couple of dollars from your local chamber of commerce.

The same type of coupon can be used in another way. Telethons are a very popular way to raise money for worthy organizations. But once the telethon is over, they have the unpleasant task of collecting the money. After the cameras are shut down, the billing goes out to collect all those pledges. To help these groups out, you could offer them a "Thank you for your pledge" coupon. This could be any kind of product and just about any kid of discount. Since they're already stuffing envelopes with the bill, it wouldn't take much more time to include your thank-you coupon. Again, this gives donors a little more for their donations. Instant gratification—and a guilt trip if they don't send the pledge in.

If you have a business that offers a general product that is needed on a regular basis, such as a restaurant, drug store, car wash, grocery store, or video arcade, the "dinner dollar" program works great. But what if you're business has a very targeted audience or is a higher ticket item?

That problem was overcome by the Nautilus Fitness Center. They didn't offer a community-service discount device because their product didn't have the mass appeal. But, it turned out that some events that were used as fund raisers were often fitness related: bikeathons, walkathons, runathons, and "so ons."

The Fitness Center manager was approached by the local Women's Bureau about being a sponsor for a 10,000 meter run fund-raising promotion. They were looking for advertisers for their program, which was a throwaway ad. The center wanted to participate in some fashion because this event was very much related to health, and both participants and spectators would be good prospects for the club.

The manager asked many questions. Part of the program was a raffle for which they needed prizes. The manager informed the rep that while he was not in a position to authorize a cash expenditure for the ad, he could authorize a free $300 membership as a prize for the raffle. Her eyes lit up.

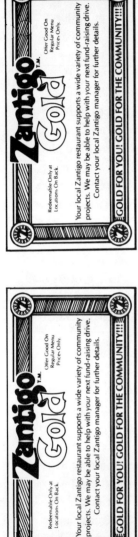

Figure 3-3

If Your Charity is Raising Money . . .
Zantigo™ Wants to Help.

Funds raised by your organization generally benefit everyone in the community. That's why Zantigo wants to help with your next fund-raising effort.

We call it "Zantigo Gold" and it works like this:

Redeemable Only at Locations On Back.

Zantigo Gold T.M.

Offer Good On Regular Menu Prices Only.

Your local Zantigo restaurant supports a wide variety of community projects. We may be able to help with your next fund-raising drive. Contact your local Zantigo manager for further details.

GOLD FOR YOU! GOLD FOR THE COMMUNITY!!!

If your group is having a Dance, Bake Sale, Raffle, Car Wash or any type of fund raiser, contact your local Zantigo Manager.

If your group qualifies, we'll issue a quantity of Zantigo Gold coupons to help your event. We'll not only provide the discount on Zantigo products, we'll even pick up the printing and paper cost for your group!

So the next time your group needs to raise money, remember . . . your local Zantigo restaurant wants to help.

Zantigo™
America's Mexican Restaurant

Figure 3-4

If You've Got a Good Cause . . . We've Got $15,000 Worth of Home Town Help.

Dear Northeast Fort Wayne Resident,

Raising funds for your neighborhood or community projects may have become increasingly difficult in recent months. If so, all of us here at Your Home Town Pizza Hut® restaurants in Northeast Fort Wayne would like to help . . . and here's how:

It's called a "Pizza Hut Buck", and as you can see from the sample, it's good for ONE DOLLAR OFF the regular menu price of any large Pizza Hut® pizza.

Whether your group is holding a Raffle, Dance, Candy Sale, Car Wash, Bazaar or other event, giving a Pizza Hut Buck with every purchase seems to remarkably increase the dollars raised!

And as our way of saying, "Thanks!" to the Northeast Fort Wayne people who have been so super to us for so long, we've set aside $15,000 worth of Pizza Hut Bucks for your fund raising projects in the coming year. To find out if your group qualifies, just contact the Manager at any Pizza Hut restaurant listed on the map on the reverse side of this page.

HELP FOR YOU, TOO!

In addition to help for your organization, we realize that "Back To School" expenses can sometimes crimp your family budget, too. So below are four great Back To School Help Coupons, redeemable at any of the three, easy to find Pizza Hut restaurants in Northeast Fort Wayne!

Figure 3-5

It's Easy to Find
YOUR HOME TOWN

Easy because there are three convenient locations right here in Northeast Fort Wayne.

- **3820 East State — State & The Bypass**
- **5801 St. Joe Road — Canterbury**
- **6039 Stellhorn Road — Northwood**

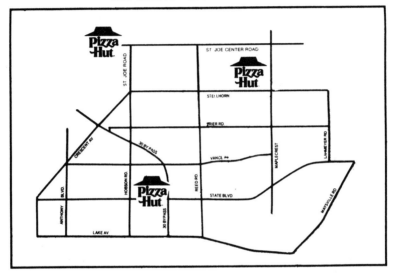

Just clip the coupons, follow the map and you're there . . . at Your Home Town Pizza Hut restaurant. Home of Pan Pizza, Thin Pizza, the famous Pizza Hut Salad Bar . . . and some real friendly folks.

Figure 3-6

71

The manager then found out that there were 50 volunteers working on the program. He offered to provide each one a free introductory membership, three visits that normally sold for $19.50. Next, they expected about 200 participants in the run. There was an entry fee, but it included one free visit to Nautilus, a $6.50 value. Last, they expected about 1,000 spectators paying admission fees, for which they received a coupon, compliments of the Women's Bureau, for 50 percent off the introductory membership.

His distribution was about 1,250 to a targeted audience. He transferred the responsibility of the discount to the Women's Bureau. He not only protected his price credibility, but established a strong *project credibility.* He didn't just offer her a bunch of coupons. He provided a special discount or membership based on the participation of the group. There were four levels of participation by the club, including the donation of the membership.

The Fitness Center was considered one of the largest contributers to the event. They provided $12,325 worth of value to the project, but their real dollar investment was only about a hundred bucks of quick printing.

Perfect Stroke with Hole-in-One Contest

Aside from coupon distribution, community involvement also allows you to capture a great deal of media coverage, which was what one streetsmart retailer recently did. He was approached by a local charity's pro/amateur celebrity golf tournament. They wanted him to become a sponsor of the event. Cost, $750, which allows you the privilege of being one of a couple of dozen or so to have a plaque displayed on the eighteenth hole. Not much visibility for your $750. He told them that he'd get back to them. He wanted to participate because it was a major event in his city. The tournament was carried live on all three local network-affiliate TV stations, and covered by the area radio stations and newspapers as well. He knew if he could somehow dominate the program, he'd get a tremendous amount of exposure and publicity, not to mention the goodwill.

When he got back to them, he told the committee that he wanted to do something extra special for this worthwhile event. He would put up $10,000 for the first golfer to get a hole-in-one on the ninth hole,

$5,000 to go to the charity and $5,000 to go to the golfer. Needless to say, they were extremely excited, and so was the press. Every TV and radio station and newspaper carried the story. Many interviewed him live on their newscasts. We had lunch with our streetfighter the day after the announcement hit, and at least five people came up to him in the restaurant to congratulate him on his contribution. The awareness and goodwill were exceedingly high.

    Then our streetfighter had a check with his logo on it enlarged for display on the ninth hole. Of course, it was one of the major topics of discussion among the golfers, and the large check was in plain view of the TV cameras every time they cut to the ninth hole.

    Was he worried that he'd have to pay up? Could all the great amount of publicity and goodwill possibly be worth $10,000 on the off-chance someone should make it? He wasn't worried. As a matter of fact, he was hoping for someone to get lucky. You see, he had purchased an insurance policy from Lloyds of London against someone making the hole-in-one on the ninth hole. The cost was $450. That's $300 less than the sponsorship! And if someone made it, that could be the best thing to happen to our streetfighter, because all that publicity would start all over again.

    You can use this same concept in your community in a number of different ways. Instead of $10,000, you could offer a car, boat, trip for two around the world, even a lifetime subscription to *Streetfighter.* (Such a deal we could make you.)

    The same idea can also be applied to other sports—like rolling a 300 game in a bowling tournament, pitching a no-hitter in a softball tournament, scoring a million points in a Pac-Man tournament, or surviving a javelin catching tournament.

Free Publicity Blossoms with Free Flowers

    If you can't find an event to dominate, create an event the way Doug Hackbarth of Broadview Florists did. He sent out a letter to all the news media announcing that any nonprofit organization wishing free flowers just had to stop to pick them up (see Figure 3-7). Almost every station carried the announcement. What was the catch? There was none. He actually was giving flowers away. It turns out that at the end of each season, there are loads of certain types of flowers, not worth

BROADVIEW FLORISTS
❀GREENHOUSES, INC.
5409 WINCHESTER ROAD, FORT WAYNE, INDIANA 46819

747-3146

July 1, 1981

FREE PLANTS FOR CHARITY

     Broadview Greenhouse has a surplus of
geraniams and bedding plants that they would like
to donate to charitable organizations such as 4-H,
hospitals, nursing homes, city park departments,
etc. . .

     For further information please contact
Doug Hackbarth at Broadview Greenhouse. Phone
747-3146

Doug Hackbarth

P.S. Please announce this as many times as
possible between now and July 10th.

Figure 3-7

It really was
a lovely thought
Thank You
for the joy it brought!

Residents of
Lutheran Homes, Inc.
Kendallville

Dear Sir,

    We want to express our appreciation
for the flowers. The residents had a
good time planning, organizing, and plant-
ing.

    It improved the appearance of the
Lutheran Home and provided some special
activity for the residents.

              Sincerely,

                Lutheran Homes, Inc.
                Kendallville, In.

Figure 3-8

their weight in mulch, destined for the scrap heap in a matter of a few weeks. So when Doug found himself with the choice between paying $50 to get them hauled away or giving them away free, he went with the freebie. A number of nursing homes jumped right on the offer. It turned out to be quite a good move for him, because since nursing homes are forever having tenant turnover, almost with the same regularity as Doug's flowers, they became good customers. He picked up some good steady customers, got rid of the soon-to-be-shrinking violets, and got the media exposure on top of it. He even received some very nice thank you cards from the recipients (see Figure 3-8).

Give a Dollar/Save a Dollar

One interesting fund-raising technique is called "give a dollar/ save a dollar." Put a fish bowl by your cash register or at your front counter. When paying their bills, your customers get the opportunity to donate a dollar to a worthy cause by placing it in the fish bowl. In doing so, they'll receive a dollar off their bill.

The key is to get the worthy organization to do all the promotion for you, which they will. They can get mentions on the local radio and TV, put up fliers, get blurbs in the paper, merchant marquees, and even announcements over the load-speaker at their school or from church pulpits. It's to their advantage to get as many people to your store as possible.

The beauty of this is that you obviously don't hand over the fistful of dollars. You write a check in the same amount as collected, which is a bottom-line tax deduction. Be sure to get a picture of you handing the check over. It makes a great publicity shot (publicity before and after).

A variation: Instead of offering a dollar off their bill this time, you give them a coupon for a dollar off on their *next* visit. In this way you get people to return at least one more time. This variation would make less of an impact on the consumer than the first would. Since it is a special event, you could combine the two. Offer the coupon as a bounce-back and transfer the responsibility of the discount to the charity.

Raising money by donating a dollar for each sale would be more of a high liability because it takes more of your time inside the store and you are donating *real dollars*. You don't want to conduct high-liability promotions all the time. Instead, look for that one or possibly two really good ones a year that can provide you with a high payoff. Ask yourself if this group will hustle and bring in a lot of customers, especially new ones. Will the promotion lend itself to publicity? Can you tie the promotion into sales by giving a dollar or a percentage of sales? Don't commit to a project right away. Wait. Find the perfect one for you. Be very selective.

Specific Item/Specific Amount

In choosing community projects, it helps to name a specific item that's needed. It could be playground equipment, softball uniforms, or medical equipment. If you can't get a specific item, then it's best to have specific amounts of money that are needed. To say, "We're helping the Girl Scouts raise money," is not as powerful as saying, "We're helping the Girl Scouts raise $650." But the ideal situation is to be able to say, "We're raising $650 to send five Girl Scouts to summer camp."

Sometimes you'll be called upon to help raise money for very expensive items for which you will be able to provide only a portion of the funds. For example, band uniforms run hundreds of dollars each. However, your contribution might be the hats. That allows you a specific item and price. Also, the hat would be more interesting than donating the right pants leg, or left spat.

The Fire Department with a Hot Promotion

The volunteer fire department was in desperate need of a deluge gun in New Haven, Indiana. The local Pizza Hut offered to donate a percentage of the gross sales on a given Wednesday. The firefighters very aggressively promoted the event. In full uniform, they brought the truck out the Saturday before—complete with Dalmations. Then, with lights flashing and siren blasting, they handed out fliers to everyone they could. They got the local media to announce the event as well. Then they put posters up—everywhere. They even put up a poster at a McDonald's down the street! Can you imagine that? What do you think would have happened if the manager of the Pizza Hut had approached McDonald's and asked to put up a poster in the store asking the patrons to eat at the competitor's down the street? The volunteers could do it, though.

When to Say Yes/How to Say No

How many times have you received a phone call that goes something like this: "Hi, Jeff. How ya doing today? (For some reason they always know your first name.) This is Woody down here at the fire department. The boys and I were just talking about you the other day. We're getting ready to put our Annual Fire Fighter's Yearbook together and wanted to know if we can count on you again this year."

As you might already know, the person calling you is really not from the local fire department, but works for a company that was hired to solicit advertising. The fire department probably gets a small fraction of the money that is raised. The person is probably calling from three states away on a WATs line in what is called a "boiler-room operation." He's one of many dozens of people sitting at a large bank of phones trying to get you to place an ad in their publication.

If you don't take the $50 ad, they always come back with a lower price, usually some odd figure like $37.50. When you reject that, they shoot you a price of $22.94. They must pull these prices out of the air. As a last-ditch effort, they'll ask you to buy a patron ad for $9.36. And when that doesn't work, many times they hang up. No goodbye. No nothing.

If it is a boiler-room operation you can turn them down without the fear of getting a less-than-positive image in the community. To determine if it is such an operation, one neat trick is tell them that it sounds like a good deal, but you'll have to talk to your supervisor or home office to get a decision. Ask for their phone number so you can get back to them.

At that point they'll say they can't wait so maybe you should wait until next year. The reason: They're not equipped to handle incoming calls. So, when they don't want to give you their number (which they can't), it's a good indication that your so-called local firefighter is sitting at a bank of phones with a number of other armchair firefighters.

One retailer we know uses a rather unique way of dealing with these calls. As you'll recall, one of the first things they say is a question, "How are you today?" This streetfighter would answer, "Not too good at all. Business is terrible. I have a million things to do and to top it off some idiot just called me to try and sell me some worthless ad in some worthless program I had no interest in whatsoever. Now, how can I help you?"

Usually about halfway through the recitation, they hang up.

Many times the requests for donations or program advertising will come from members of your community. You don't want to get a negative image in the community, so you have to be careful. The ideal way to handle these requests is to direct them to someone else—an advertising agency, home office, or area supervisor. Tell them that those decisions are made elsewhere and give them the number. If you can give them a long-distance number, you'll get rid of half the requests right away. And notice, you didn't turn them down. Someone else will.

There might come a time when you have to deal with the request yourself. Here's a way that we found to be very effective. First, listen to their pitch all the way through. But before you go into your stock turndown routine, make sure there is no real opportunity in it for you—which will be the case most of the time. Once you determine that it would be a throwaway ad tell them, "Gee, that sounds like a tremendous program, and I would really like to help you. But here's my problem. We set aside a budget at the beginning of our fiscal year for just such worthy programs. Unfortunately, the budget is all used up this year. Perhaps if you could get to us earlier next year we could help you out. Thanks for calling."

You're not saying no. As a matter of fact, it sounds like you want to participate, it's just that they contacted you at the wrong time. The amateur salesperson asking for the donation doesn't feel rejected, because he or she convinced you it was a worthwhile program, so you maintain your good-guy image.

By next year, committees change, people move, and when it's time for you to get your phone call from that group again, it will probably be another person, so you can use the same story once again.

In all the years that we've been using this approach, we've only been caught once. A woman representing a high school varsity football team called up and asked that a restaurant client of ours buy a $37 program ad. We went through our stock routine just like the one mentioned. She called back about 20 minutes later and said she had just talked to the coach, who informed her that their team last year had had two different banquets at that restaurant (one for $400 and one for $700). "Would you like to reconsider?" she asked.

It sounded like she had us, and we knew we would have to buy the ad, but our response was one that helped maintain credibility. "We see your point. We're not authorized to approve the ad, but because of the unique circumstances, we will call the owner and see if he will make an exception. We'll call you back in a couple of hours with his decision."

Without ever making the call, we set an alarm watch for two hours, and then we called her back to tell her that her ad had been approved.

So, even if on the off chance you do get taken by surprise using this approach to handling a public service request, you can somewhat gracefully get out of it by some quick thinking.

One other way to avoid having to buy an ad is to ask when they need the artwork. It's usually due in two or three days. That's your out. Tell them that you would really like to help them out, but it takes at least two weeks to produce an ad, then it must be run by the legal department at the corporate offices, which takes another three to four weeks. "Maybe if you come back a little earlier next year."

Converting Promotions into Community Involvement

Many times you'll run promotions for your business that, with a small modification, could be turned into a viable service to the community. That lets you tap into free media coverage, as well as generating goodwill and getting the hands and feet of the members of the organization you're working with.

T-Shirt Trade-In

Businesses that give away T-shirts at various events without a doubt generate a great deal of excitement. It's an item that costs anywhere from $4 to $8 and it has your advertising on it. But instead of giving the shirts away, require that they trade in an old shirt for the new one. We call this the *Great T-Shirt Trade-In.* Then all the old shirts are washed and donated to a worthwhile organization that will see that they find their way into the hands of the needy. It costs you no more to add this twist, but you'll have a good chance to get media coverage and marketing help from the nonprofit organization.

The same idea could be done by a number of different types of businesses. Take for example, retail eyeglasses. You could run a sale on single-lens glasses at a low price to build foot traffic. If you price the glasses ridiculously low and run it for a one-day-only promotion, you can create a great deal of impact. But take that same promotion and require that people trade in an old pair of glasses, any kind and any condition, for the new Eyeglass. Call it the *Great Eyeglass Trade-In.* Then all the old glasses can be donated to underprivileged people. Again, it costs you no more to advertise and makes the low price more believable. A perfect sponsor might be the local Lions Club because they're already heavily involved in programs concerning eyes and blindness.

Look for opportunity. Where there is a need, help a group fill that need. Would it cost you any more to require that customers trade in a piece of old merchandise for new? No. Whether it's an old T-shirt, eyeglasses, dishes, shoes, toys, or whatever you want to put on sale, think in terms of helping others while you help yourself.

Getting a Premium out of a Premium

Self-liquidating premiums are often used to increase foot traffic. These items are provided at a very low cost when you purchase a specific item or service. To be truly self-liquidating, the price you get for the item should be what it costs you (including the point-of-purchase displays and other advertising involved with the promotion). Almost anything can be used. Some of the most common are drinking glasses, blankets, silverware, dishes, and calculators.

But while offering these premiums may increase foot traffic, it usually requires that you advertise heavily in the mass media. Even then, many of the recipients will be your own customers. But there is a way to use a premium to bring in new customers.

A restaurant was running a cooler promotion. The cost of the cooler was $2 with the purchase of any dinner. Then, for the next six months, you could bring your cooler in and if you bought a dinner, they'd fill the cooler with a beverage, free. This kept the customers coming back time and time again.

The first year this was done, the coolers were sold inside the store. But the following year they used a little street savvy. The program was done with the local Boy Scouts.

A couple of weeks before the cooler would go on sale for $2, the Scouts took them door-to-door and sold them for $3. The kids had to tell the people that the coolers would be available in a couple of weeks for $2 and a purchase from a restaurant, but by buying now, the extra dollar would go to the Boy Scouts. Also, by buying now they would receive a $2 coupon for their next dinner. Then the Boy Scouts paid $2 for each of the coolers they sold. They could return the unsold ones— but there weren't any!

They had sold over 500 coolers. But, more important, the people who bought the coolers from the Scouts, as opposed to inside the store, had a much higher possibility of being *new* customers. And there was was the added advantage of not having the cashier mess around with them at the counter.

Your Friendly Neighborhood Tour Guide

Providing tours for schools or church groups is a great way to get involved at very little cost. Many teachers like to take their kids on field trips. If you can get them to bring their kids to your operation, the kids often bug their parents to take them there again. It makes a very big impact. Now, if you have a Hot Sam pretzel franchisee in a mall with 20 square feet, it might be a problem. But any type of retail operation where things are being made would be of great interest to young children.

To set these up, send a letter to the teachers to let them know. Be sure to stress what the kids will learn. You also might send a release to the media, and especially the teacher's union. They'll have some kind of newsletter that is sent to all the members. To get the most out of this effort, provide the kids with a goody-bag containing some inexpensive toys and candy. As part of the bag, include a coupon for the parents (see Figure 3-9).

Figure 3-9

Last, whenever you help an organization, be sure to ask for a letter of thanks. Many of them will send one to you anyway. A letter of thanks is a nice touch. Have it reduced and printed at your local quick printer, and use it as a bag stuffer or statement stuffer. As long as you're getting the goodwill, make sure your regular customers are aware of the nice things you're doing for the community. It reinforces that they made the right choice in buying from you.

On the Other Side of the Pence

Should you find yourself on the other side of a community-involvement program, remember to create the "everyone wins" situation. Many of us are involved in our own organizations and we're called on to help with fund raisers. The best ones are ones where the merchants will get some real benefits besides a tax write-off for a donation. Instead of asking for money, it's much easier to get merchandise and then hold an auction, raffle, Monte Carlo, or bingo game. When selling tickets, get a restaurant or possibly a car wash to provide you with some version of the "dinner dollar." And always let them know that you'll try to get as much publicity for them as possible in this event. They'll understand the value of that.

A great story of a streetfighting volunteer is that of Barbra Burton of Cincinnati, Ohio. She had long been a disciple of streetfighting and wanted the information to help her in a number of nonprofit activities. No efforts compare with hers to create public awareness in her community for wearing seatbelts and using restraining devices for infants (see Figure 3-10).

Aside from getting fifteen billboards donated, free commercial time, and editorial time in the media, she was able to set up a distribution system for circulating over 50,000 brochures. She set it up like a cross-promotion, which included distribution from a chain of 35 gas stations and a chain of 30 grocery stores, plus hospitals, clinics and so on.

She got the artwork and photography through a local high-school art department. The students volunteering their time received credit for their efforts and something for their portfolios. She even got the printing donated by asking local printers each to print a few thousand. (The printers were donating product-cost dollars.)

Figure 3-10

She was able to achieve this tremendous success by creating the everyone-wins situation and by understanding what it would take to get each person she dealt with to cooperate.

Winning Over Your Community

When you look at streetsmart community involvement, look at it as another means of free distribution of your advertising message. That distribution could be door-to-door in the form of a coupon or a live announcement by a Cub Scout. It could be an announcement in the media about an upcoming event, or a feature story about how you helped raise a specific amount of money for a very needed item in your community.

You have to look at the payback for your efforts, and you have to consider how our involvement in charitable projects helps set you apart from your competition. Create the everyone-wins situation and you'll be a winner every time.

4

In-Store Marketing

From the Front Door to the Cash Register

"Small improvements on existing successful programs"—this is one of the main principles of streetfighting. But though it's important to all aspects of streetfighting, this concept is practically the underlying theme of in-store marketing. It's truly amazing how just one concept can often be improved, modified, adapted, or otherwise altered to create an entirely different use—a use that's designed to bring you new customers, or to get additional sales from existing ones.

Advertising can only get potential customers to call or visit your store. It can't sell the merchandise or service. That has to be done by you or your employees. Customers may cross your threshold, but you still have to get them to the cash register before you can make a profit.

With cross-promotions, you looked at the two- or three-mile radius around your store. With community involvement and publicity, the radius can be expanded to include the entire city. But with in-store marketing, your efforts become introverted. Small improvements are credited that allow you to conduct cross-promotions with yourself, to generate internal publcity and goodwill, to look for opportunities that are within arms reach.

Turning the Maintenance Person into a Sales Person

Contests can be fun, and when they are, you'll get a much greater response from them than from giving an order, creating a new policy, or circulating a memo. The suggested-sell contest is done with all of your salespeople. When we refer to salespeople, we mean anyone who has the opportunity to get a customer to buy. In the food service business it would be waiters and waitresses; in bars, taverns, and night clubs it would be the bartender; in a drug store it might be the pharmacist or checkout person; in retail it could be the floor clerk or counter person. Each of these people is in direct contact with the customer once that customer has entered your establishment. They each have the opportunity to influence that customer to buy more, creating incremental sales for you—sales that otherwise would have been lost or gone to a competitor.

To run a suggested-sell contest, first determine what it is you wish to sell more of. Remember, it should be an item that will provide *incremental* sales. The contest could be used to get people to step up to more expensive or more profitable models. It could be accessories or it could be necessities. The owner of a Jeremiah Sweeny's restaurant wanted to push cream pies. The manager of a Pizza Hut wanted to suggest their Super Supreme Pizza. At Trevor True Value Hardware it was light bulbs. At the Parker Shelton School of Karate it was a family add-on membership. None of these items was originally considered by the customer. But because of the suggestion of the person in charge, each store was able to pick up additional dollars and profit. Not an expensive "sell" either—just a kind word, a helpful comment.

The Rules

The contest should be very simple. First, you need to pick a given period of time the contest is to run. Depending on your type of business and the product you're trying to suggest-sell, you might want to run it a week or two, but usually no longer than a month. Longer than a month and it begins to lose its impact on your people.

Next, you need prizes. You can use anything, but it's best to use products that are *not* from your own store. This really makes the contest appear to be special. To get the prizes, try trading for them by approaching other merchants in your area. Ask them if they've ever considered running an employee contest. They'll probably tell you no. So you say, "We never did either, but now we thought we might try it." Then say that you'd like to trade retail dollar for retail dollar, your merchandise for theirs. Record albums, dinners, movie passes, car washes, clocks, and many other items are good candidates for prizes. You still may need to buy a grand prize, but that needn't be too expensive. In the case of the Jeremiah Sweeny's franchisee we mentioned earlier, the grand prize was the chance to throw one of their famous cream pies in the owner's face. That seemed to be one of the most motivating prizes yet.

Does it work? Again the Jeremiah Sweeny's example turned out to be very profitable. Not only did they triple pie sales during the month of the contest, they even noticed a 20 percent residual increase long after the contest was over. So much excitement was created about the contest that some waitresses were even selling whole pies to go—something that was never even thought of before this event. Some of their regular customers were even helping their favorite waitresses to get new customers to buy pie. But the reason they showed an overall increase in pie sales long after the contest ended was that the waitresses found out just how easy it was to "sell" them. Not only that, but by building that guest check up with some extra desserts, their 15-percent tip was built up as well.

Tips on Tipping

While we're on the subject of tipping, let's digress for a moment and discuss some strategies on how to get more tips. Even though your particular business may not use help that gets tips, the information here is a valuable lesson on "perceived value" and will give you an interesting insight as to how the mind works. We found this to be so fascinating that we just had to find a place to tell you about it. In-store marketing seemed to be the logical chapter.

We were consulting a nightclub and found a waitress who consistently got larger tips than all of the other waitresses. Her service was good, but nothing exceptional. As a matter of fact, we thought some of the others were better. Yet, this woman still raked it in night after night. After watching her for some time and figuring out nothing, we finally asked her what she was doing.

First she told us that whenever she gave change she made it easy for the customer to leave a tip. If the change was $5 and some-odd cents, she would give four quarters and four singles. We figured that was just common sense; it really didn't impress us much.

Then she told us that in giving change, she always returns the money face down, whether coin or paper. It appears to be less valuable that way. We were confused!

She told us to take out a couple of dollars and lay them on the table in front of us, one face down and the other face up. We did. For some reason, the bill placed face down did appear to be less valuable than the other. Odd.

She then told us that she prefers to leave old worn-out money instead of crisp new bills. Furthermore, she never places the change on the table, but always returns it on her serving tray. This forces the customer to deal with the change at that moment. It also puts some pressure on the customer because he or she has to deal with the change in front of friends, clients, and the waitress.

The coins are placed flat on the serving tray, never overlapping. This makes them more difficult to pick up. Many times the customer will leave the coins instead of dealing with them and appearing to be a tightwad. The paper money is then placed, face down of course, on top of the change, with the lowest denomination on the bottom and the highest on the top. When she extends the serving tray to the customer, she holds it about shoulder height, which makes it a little more awkward to pick up the change.

After her little lecture we realized that she had it down to a science. She had to. That's how she made her living. We told her how impressed we were with her information. She then picked up the two dollars we had placed on the table in front of us, thanked us, and walked away. We never forgot her lesson!

Getting Your Employees to Bring You New Customers

With the suggested-sell contest, you're limited to just the people who are in direct contact with customers. But with a small improvement, you're able to turn your entire staff into streetfighters, and they'll have fun doing it. It's called an *employee incentive contest* and it works like this: Each employee—both full- and part-time—gets a number of cards, say 50, similar to the examples in Figures 4-1 and 4-2. They can get more if they so desire.

This entitles your employees' friends to a special discount of some

NOW YOU HAVE A FRIEND
IN THE FLOWER BUSINESS!

This card entitles the bearer to a **20% DISCOUNT**
on his or her next purchase of a foliage plant or hanging basket.

Courtesy of ______________________________

CASH AND CARRY ONLY
Offer Expires September 30, 1981

BROADVIEW

FLORIST • GREENHOUSE • LANDSCAPING

5409 WINCHESTER ROAD • FORT WAYNE, IN 46819 • 747-3146

Figure 4-1

BRING A FRIEND TO PIZZA HUT®
FOR LUNCH,
AND WE'LL FEED YOUR FRIEND
FOR HALF PRICE!

Buy one of our delicious Lunch Combinations at the regular menu price, and your friend can buy one of equal value for HALF-PRICE! 11 am to 3 pm, M-F.

VALID ONLY THROUGH MARCH 31, 1982 AND ONLY AT:

Your Home Town Pizza Hut.

The East State Pizza Hut®
restaurant

3820 East State at The Bypass
Fort Wayne, Indiana Phone 483-9531

Authorized By ______________________

Figure 4-2

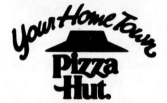

kind in your store. The more you need the business, the higher the discount. The card also has a place for an authorized signature. This is where the employee signs the card. Not only does signing the card and authorizing a special discount make the employee feel special and important, but it also transfers the responsibility of the discount. That discount is not perceived as an ongoing program. Rather, it's a discount only made available under a special set of circumstances, ,knowing somebody on the "inside." One of the most important rules is that they can't pass out the coupons in the store. It must be done on their own time.

Results can be figured in a couple of ways. You can either count the number of cards redeemed per person, or include the amount of the entire gross sale. When using the gross-sale method, the redeemed card is attached to the sales slip or guest check. The total gross sale is recorded as that employee's contribution to the contest, and the employee with the highest gross sale wins. This forces the employees to think a little. They could pass the cards out to friends who might come in and just buy the discount items. But if you use the total-gross-sales method, they're more inclined to pass them out to people who will buy a lot more than the discounted items. Like someone who is shopping for their entire family.

The neat thing about this particular promotion is that it involves all of your employees—clerical, bookkeepers, dishwashers, mechanics, and even the janitor. Not only are you getting coupons distributed free, but you're subtly getting a recommendation from your employees, their friend—an organized form of word-of-mouth advertising.

The card also has an expiration date, just like a coupon. This protects you from having to discount beyond the contest. Again, prizes are traded just like the suggested-sell contest.

Customer Cloning

Yet another small improvement to the employee incentive program is customer cloning. This one gets your customers to bring in new customers. There are a couple of applications of the concept. The first is the "buddy pass" (see Figures 4-3 and 4-4).

GUEST PASS

Parker Shelton Judo & Karate

GUEST MEMBER____________________________________
IS ENTITLED TO **50%** OFF THE REGULAR PRICE OF THE INTRODUCTORY LESSONS. YOU SAVE $9.75.

INCLUDES:

- SELF DEFENSE
- SUN TAN BOOTH
- SAUNA & STEAM BOOTH
- WEIGHT TRAINING
- BODY CONDITIONING
- COMPETITION

GUEST OF____________ RANK____________ **"Be The Best"**
If under 18 years of age must be accompanied by parent.

Figure 4-3

In club-type operations your customers are also members and can be very helpful in bringing you more of the same. When they sign up at your club, you'll find that their greatest enthusiasm is during that first month. So that's when you have to get their help.

Both of these clubs use a special introductory membership program. Their regular memberships run hundreds of dollars a year. When most people hear that amount over the phone they don't show·

Guest Pass

ALL SPORTS FITNESS CENTER

Nautilus

Name ________________________________
Phone ________________________________
This pass entitles the above person to 50% off one introductory week (valued at $19.50, a savings of $9.75). Good for up to three visits.
Compliments of ____________________________

Offer Expires____/____/____

3602 SOUTH CALHOUN (Across from South Side) • (219) 456-1956
OPEN SIX DAYS A WEEK • CALL FOR AN APPOINTMENT

Figure 4-4

up for an appointment. Also, it's a fairly large commitment on the part of the prospect, especially since they don't know if they're going to like it or not. To deal with this, a program that allows prospects to try the program for a limited time for a small amount of money was instituted. The karate school gives five lessons for $19.50, and the Nautilus club allows three workouts for $19.50.

Once they get individuals involved in the program, they start the selling process to get the prospects on as members. Once converted to full membership, each person is handed three or four buddy passes, and can get more if they need them. This allows them to bring their friends in to try the program at 50 percent of the introductory rate. The karate school uses both half-off and free passes depending on how slow business is. Again, the purpose of the intro is to get prospects involved in the program so they can be converted to a full membership.

Note that when clubs discount, they seldom discount their regular program, only the *introductory* membership. This allows them to get the full price on the regular membership.

When a friend of a member signs up for a regular program, the member gets something. In the karate school, it's a cash incentive. In the Nautilus club, it's a free month added on to their membership. Both work well, but of course the free month means less out-of-pocket.

The Contest

The buddy pass program is ongoing—week in and week out, but once a year or so, the clubs improve the concept again with a membership drive contest. The buddy passes are used, and the regular incentives are in place as always, but some added incentives make it more competitive. The person who brings in the most buddies that month wins the grand prize. A stereo, color TV, cash, and a trip have all been used for these contests over the years. There are also second- and third-place prizes and a few more runner-up prizes, too. The clubs required a minimum of three new members to qualify for the contest, so the risk was very low: One qualifier and the contest paid for itself, the rest was gravy.

Not only did this create more excitement in the clubs, and generate new members, but the people who have been around for five years made a little more effort to bring in new members at this time.

Fix My Friend

The modifications of existing successful programs continue with yet another customer incentive program. This one was used by 20th Century Automotive. When a regular customer came in to pick up their car or truck, the counterperson handed them a couple of 10 percent discount coupons (see Figure 4-5).

A regular customer who brought three new customers to the shop would receive a free-oil-change card (see Figure 4-6). This little program brought in a great deal of new cutomers and the cost was practically nil. In most cases, your customers are glad to tell their friends about your store. (See Figure 4-7 for another idea.)

In one of his seminars, Murray Raphel, coauthor of *The Great Brain Robbery* (self-published), tells the story of the owner of a major construction company who was playing golf with the president of a bank. The bank president turned to his friend and said, "You know, we've been playing golf together for a long time now. How come you've never put any money in my bank?"

The construction company president simply replied, "You never asked me."

SAVE A FRIEND 10%
at 20TH CENTURY AUTOMOTIVE

1001 LEESBURG ROAD • FORT WAYNE, INDIANA

MY FRIEND_____
    WOULD LIKE TO SAVE 10% ON THIS AUTOMOTIVE REPAIR.
    APPLIES TO LABOR ONLY. PARTS NOT INCLUDED.
    CANNOT BE COMBINED WITH ANY OTHER DISCOUNT
        OR SPECIAL OFFER
RECOMMENDED BY_____ DATE___/___/___
    CALL FOR AN APPOINTMENT 432-5325

"IF WE CAN'T FIX IT, IT CAN'T BE FIXED!"

Figure 4-5

FREE OIL CHANGE
The bearer of this card is entitled to ONE FREE OIL CHANGE including 5 quarts of oil, oil filter and labor at:

20th Century Automotive

1001 Leesburg Road • Fort Wayne, Indiana
"If we can't fix it, it can't be fixed!"
Call for an appointment 432-5325.
Authorized by________________ Expires ___/___/___

Figure 4-6

Besides referral programs and internal contests, there are a number of things you can do without leaving the store that can help sales. We were asked by an appliance dealer to help them solve a problem. Their customers were shopping them to death. They'd come in, get a price then tell the salesperson they wanted to think about it—which means they were going to a dozen other places to shop for the best price. In too many of the cases, they were never seen again. The first thing we did was to create a simple folder. Customers shopping for high-ticket items are usually handed a full-color flier provided by the manufacturer and rubber-stamped with the dealer's name. Then they take all of these fliers home to study the costs, features, and so on. Our folder had the appliance store logo on both the front and back covers. On the inside was the usual propaganda about the service department, helpful staff, and so on. The right side contained a flap for inserting the brochures and was die cut so the salesperson could insert a business card. The purpose of the folder was to allow this appliance store to dominate the others.

As it turned out, it did a little more than that. Not only did the client's brochures get inserted into the folder, but since it was so convenient, many times the competition's brochures were inserted as well. On a couple of occasions, people returned to the appliance store wanting to buy the wrong merchandise! Of course, they were quickly reminded of the benefits of the brand the store did carry.

MAKE ME POUR, AND I'LL MAKE YOU $25 RICHER!

If you give me a lead on a new account - - new cups to pour my delicious coffee, tea and hot chocolate into --I'll reward you with $25. Just introduce me to a potential client who will use at least one box of coffee a month, (approx. 8 regular drinkers) and as soon as they place their first order, I'll place $25 in front of you. One new client, one box of coffee a month . . . one nice bonus, just for you.

Call Executive Coffee Service 432-6712

Figure 4-7

Icing Competitive Price Shopping

Even with the success of the folder, we recommended one other little program. We had them fill one of their freezers with half-gallons of ice cream. When a customer was ready to leave, but not to buy, the sales staff was instructed to give them one of these containers of ice cream. A free present for stopping in. No strings attached. The customers hearts melted at this gesture of goodwill, and they left with a very good feeling about this appliance store.

By the time they got to their car on a very hot July day, their hearts weren't the only things melting. When the ice cream was placed on the seat next to them, it had already started to drip ever so slightly—enough to motivate many bargain-hunters to retreat to their home where they could place the rapidly melting box of summer delight safely in their freezer. Once their shopping spree was interrupted and the momentum broken, they many times just couldn't psych themselves up to go out again, and our good-humor appliance dealer was able to scoop up a little extra business.

All the Store's a Stage

Another aspect of in-store marketing is the appearance of the store. This is very important especially during a major promotion or sale. A fabric and yarn shop decided to have a warehouse sale, but the inside of the store looked the same as it did any other day. No believability for the sale.

When you're going to have a desperation sale of some kind, you have to make the store look like you're desperate. One store had all the merchandise displayed in neat little rows, and everything was orderly. We had them take the order out of the store. We have expertise in the area of marketing, advertising, and sales promotions, and we know that nothing compares with taking the order out of an orderly place. You need only visit our offices to see just how effective we are at this very intricate technique.

First, we had them cram their 5,000-square-foot store down to 1,200 square feet. To make this scene of the incredible shrinking store believable, tarps were placed in the unused areas of the store along with a few ladders and a couple of empty cans of Pabst Blue Ribbon. Now we had a real reason for the sale—remodeling. "Remodeling?" the client inquired. "Sure," we said. "When it's all over, paint one of the walls."

Now, with all this merchandise squeezed into such a small space, it really looked like you could pick up some bargains. Much of the stuff was stacked in cases and presented a definite air of chaos. It was a thing of beauty and very believable.

A jewelry shop had a bunch of $3 necklaces they couldn't move. The necklaces were neatly stacked in individual boxes behind the glass case. We suggested that the clerks remove the necklaces from the boxes and place them in a pile on a card table in front of the glass cases. Then a sign was placed on the table that read "Marked Down to $4." They were sold out in a couple of weeks.

Perceived value is more important than the real value in selling merchandise. If people truly believe they're getting a good deal, they'll buy. If they feel that it's not a good value, even if you're charging half of what it's really worth, they won't buy. What's important is the value that the customer *believes* is the value. In the nightclub business we always ask our clients which they think is a better value, a two-for-the-price-of-one beer or beer at half-off. They both cost the same and generate the same profit margin. The answers seem to lean toward the two-for-one. First of all, the two-for-one deals with the amount of product, not the price. Customers get twice as much for their money, which seems to be a very powerful tool. Also, since they get two beers at the same time, they tend to drink faster because they don't want to let that beer get too warm. Another advantage is that it puts more money through the register and is less work for the waitresses. But the biggest thing is it gets customers to buy more.

Partners in Lime

With all the referral programs we've mentioned, one has yet to be discussed. This is one where your competitor refers your business. Sound odd? This happened to a group of nightclubs. Five of them teamed up with the following idea. In a business where many people go bar-hopping, they decided to work together to get the people hopping among their bars and not the couple of dozen other major competitors. When customers would leave, the doorkeeper would hand them a coupon good for a two-for-one drink available at any of the other six bars mentioned on the coupon. It was good that night only. The responsibility of the discount was transferred to the Bar Owner's Association, which they had formed and paid money into to cover the expense of printing the coupons. Coupons were color coded

Compliments of the United Allen County Bar Owners Association.

TWO FOR ONE

The bearer of this card is entitled to one free drink with the purchase of an identical drink at the regular price. Cannot be combined with any other discount or special. Good at:

Shenanigan's	**Poor Johns**
Brickly's Firehouse	**The Scorpion**
Grady's Place	**Denny's VIP Lounge**
Cagney's Pub	

Figure 4-8

so they could see exactly where their new customers were coming from (see Figure 4-8).

One nightclub in particular did some very successful promotions. When they did these promotions, they gave a great amount of attention to the facilities themselves, as well as to the marketing and advertising. For example, they once had a prom night. All the employees wore tuxedos, and the customers were given gifts: corsages for the women, boutonnieres for the men. The formal wear and flowers were traded out for mentions in the advertising. The entire club was decorated like a high-school prom, complete with a nerf basketball hoop on the dance floor with minature balloons in the net. The customers walked in through an arch. A prom queen and prom king were chosen, and she was given a dozen roses (traded of course). There was a snow-ball dance, a special spiked punch, and a photographer to take pictures of couples, many of whom showed up in formal wear. Then the club was shut down an hour early for an after-prom party for all the employees.

The front door opening for your promotion or sale should be like the curtain going up on opening night of a Broadway play.

In-store marketing can also incorporate general sales techniques. A client of Larry Halt, of Sales Acceleration, Inc., uses a pretalk book in a drugstore. This technique is usually used by salespeople in direct calls. A good pretalk book is a visual aid that guides the prospect through a sales pitch. Not only does it serve as a visual aid, but it also helps the salesperson stay on the right track during the pitch. The first few pages are devoted to some interesting facts about their particular industry, usually trying to bring out any objections a prospect has. Then it goes on to explain about the organization and then about the products.

Halt's drugstore client adapted this idea. They placed their pretalk book on a stand in front of the counter where the prescriptions are filled. Often there's a waiting line and people get very anxious. Many times, if the line is long, they'll leave and go elsewhere for their prescriptions.

The pretalk book was placed on a stand like those found in funeral homes to put the Bible on. Customers waiting in line for their prescriptions to be filled would start leafing through this book. Soon they would be reminded that they needed aspirin or toothpaste or whatever.

Not only did this idea keep people from getting too bored and leaving, but it also allowed the store to sell more products to them by merely suggesting the idea.

Signs Sell

The same idea applies to signs. They really do help sell more merchandise. A number of years ago we conducted some research for a grocery store company. They had two stores in the same town doing like volumes. Then, one store placed signs everywhere suggesting that people buy various products. The other store remained as it was with no signs. The store with signs did 5 percent more volume than the one without. When you consider the volume that a grocery store does, this was very significant.

If you have an item that you really want to push, push it with signs. You can have your counter and floor personnel wear buttons to suggest special buys as well.

If you run an ad in the newspaper, take it to your local quick printer and have them provide you a film positive or PMT of the ad. They can usually go up as high as 11 by 17 inches. This will be a black-and-white glossy of your ad, which you then mount on a colored art board with at least two or three inches for a border. Instant poster. If you need only a couple of them, this is the cheapest and fastest way to do it.

Once again, if you get an article in the local newspaper, take it to the local quick printer and have it blown up on a film positive. Mount it down. It looks great in your store and reminds your regulars what a great store it is.

Stuff It, Fella ...

When customers leave they should take with them something about your store. Never overlook the opportunity for promoting yourself to your existing customers. Fliers used as bag stuffers are very effective. If you have a new service that you offer or a new product you want to make them aware of, put it on a flier and stuff it in the bag. They have to open the bag to get the merchandise out anyway. At the very least, you'll make an impression while your ad is on the way to the wastebasket.

If you want publicity about your store, again, reprint a news item on a flier and stuff it in the bag. As we mentioned in the chapter on publicity, publicity that is not advertising helps give you credibility. Also, there might be regular customers who didn't see that particular news item. So, make sure they see it by bag-stuffing it. (See Figure 4-9 for example.)

Bag-stuffing is a very inexpensive way to advertise to your customers. Aside from general publicity, you can make fliers to announce upcoming promotions or sales, or to promote a new line of merchandise or a new service.

A variation of the bag-stuffer can be used by dry cleaners, tailors, or clothing stores. When a hanger is used, you can print a small flier on card stock and have a hole drilled toward the top to slip it right on the hanger. This small improvement is called the "hanger hanger."

Printing with a Secondary Purpose

One of the most effective forms of in-store marketing is used by some Pizza Hut franchisees—primarily those who attended our

CHINA SALE NOTICE

You are a special customer of WATKINS so we would like to offer you the first opportunity to save 20 to 40% on all of our fine china.

On Sunday, April 19, an ad in the Paducah Sun will announce this savings to the public. This gives you just a little time to take advantage of the huge selection and great savings

Plus, use the WATKINS china gift certificate for an additional savings of $5.00 on purchases of $25.00 or more.

HURRY TO WATKINS TODAY!

Watkins
422 Broadway
443-4571

Figure 4-9

seminars. They use a placemat. They have to use a placemat anyway, so the additional cost to use them to promote events is nonexistent.

In addition, they have a captive audience for a few minutes—

until the pizza arrives. What else can the customers do while they're waiting, with the possible exceptions of looking out the window or checking out the socks on the guy in the next booth? But with the placemat, they now have something to do that's more interesting than counting the number of holes in the acoustical tile.

The back side of the placemat has games for the kiddies, and the front side is a great medium for advertising various promotions (see Figures 4-10, 4-11, and 4-12). They're so effective that some radio and TV stations have traded air time in exchange for exposure on the placemat.

The same program could be done with tray liners for fast food operations. Most of the larger operations are provided with liners. But usually you can get them blank with just the border and the logo at the top. Then it's just a matter of over-printing with your message for that week.

So effective is this technique that we wanted to find a way to adapt the idea for the nightclub client. They didn't serve food (except for a cheese sandwich for $29.95. In this particular state there's a law that requires all bars to serve food, but it doesn't dictate the price they can charge).

Their adaptation of the placemat was the beverage coaster. This was a simple four-inch-square piece of printed card stock. The border remained the same every week, but the message inside changed weekly. They used it to announce special events or ongoing programs like happy hour (Figures 4-13 and 4-14). Again, they're so effective that a local stereo dealer gave the club a $600 car stereo to be used in a contest at the club in exchange for mentions on their coasters.

The odd thing about it was that the coasters replaced regular cocktail napkins and table tents. The napkins had a simple black logo imprint that never changed. The table tents never seemed to last past the first round of drinks. But with coasters, every time a customer was served another drink, another coaster was slapped down on the table in front of them. Every time he or she would take a drink, it would draw more and more attention to the message on the coaster. But even more interesting, the customized coasters saved the club about one-hundred dollars a month. When the waiters or waitresses would spill a drink, they were forced to use a bar towel to clean it up instead of a dozen expensive napkins.

Your Home Town Pizza Hut®

The Home Town All You Can Eat...

SUNDAY BUFFET!

Every Sunday 11 AM - 2 PM

It's a special treat for you to take advantage of right after church!

It's all the Pizza, Pasta, Salad Bar and Bread Sticks you can eat for one low price. Plus, it's just HALF-PRICE for children under 10. So bring the entire family!

In addition, there will be FREE REFILLS on all soft beverages!

So mark it down . . . and make it a date. This Sunday and every Sunday at Your Home Town Pizza Hut® restaurant.

Sunday Buffet currently available at this Pizza Hut® restaurant only.

ALL YOU CAN EAT
$3.99

(Children Under 10 **HALF PRICE**)

Figure 4-10

104

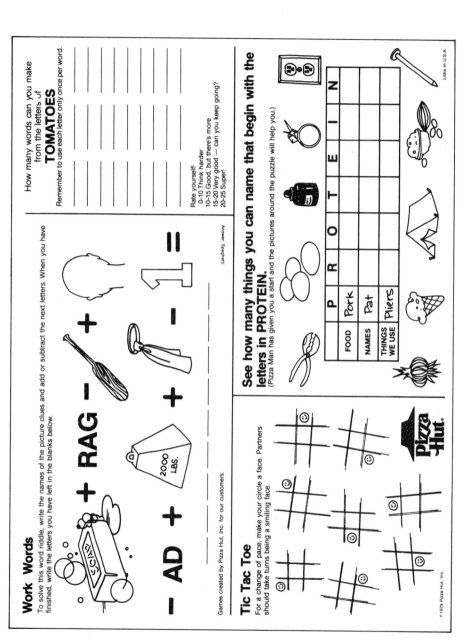

Work Words

To solve this word riddle, write the names of the picture clues and add or subtract the next letters. When you have finished, write the letters you have left in the blanks below.

+ RAG −

+ − 1 =

− AD +

_____

Answer: Spaghetti

Games created by Pizza Hut, Inc. for our customers.

Tic Tac Toe

For a change of pace, make your circle a face. Partners should take turns being a smiling face.

© 1979 Pizza Hut, Inc.

How many words can you make
from the letters of
TOMATOES

Remember to use each letter only once per word.

_____
_____
_____
_____
_____
_____
_____
_____
_____
_____
_____
_____
_____
_____
_____

Rate yourself!
0-10 Think harder
10-15 Good, but there's more
15-20 Very good — can you keep going?
20-25 Super!

See how many things you can name that begin with the letters in PROTEIN.

(Pizza Man has given you a start and the pictures around the puzzle will help you.)

	P	R	O	T	E	I	N
FOOD	Pork						
NAMES	Pat						
THINGS WE USE	Pliers						

Litho in U.S.A.

Figure 4-11

105

Now
15" Pan Pizza

Comin' in for good

Pizza Hut®

From the day we first introduced Pan Pizza, we knew we had a winner. And we were right — just about everyone took a liking to it.

Well, now for all you Pan Pizza fans, we're pleased to announce that you can order your favorite Pan Pizza in our big 15" size.

To order the size that's right for you: a 9" Pan Pizza serves 2 to 3 people, a 13" serves 3 to 4, and the new 15" Pan Pizza serves 5 to 6 hungry pizza eaters.

So order it to dine in or get one to go. Either way, it's a crowd pleaser.

Figure 4-12

Figure 4-13

Figure 4-14

The Gift that Keeps on Selling

Gift certificates are also good in-store marketing programs. There are two types: predetermined amounts, like the kind that McDonald's uses around Christmastime, with each one worth 50 cents; and open amounts, the kind on which you write in the amount of the gift, like a check.

These are incremental sales. They also serve as a good replacement for currency when trying to arrange trades. Another advantage is that they are prepayment on merchandise yet to be sold. And best of all, many companies that sell them tell us they get as high as 20 percent slippage; that is, up to 20 percent of all certificates sold never get redeemed!

You Open the Register Only to Close the Sale

With all these in-store marketing programs, there is still no replacement for good solid sales ability. If you have a person on the phone, on the floor, or on the counter who can sell, they're worth their weight in sales slips.

Closing the sale is what it's all about. An apartment complex in Florida used a very interesting closing technique to turn their lookers into leasers. A prospect would come in and get the pitch. If at any time they looked as if there might be the slightest difficulty closing, the leasing agent would pop herself in the head (as if to say, "I could have had a V-8") and say, "I almost forgot. We're running a contest this week." She then would go over to a large fishbowl filled with folded pieces of paper. "On each of those pieces of paper is a dollar amount, $2, $4, $6, $8, and some that are even $10. You can draw out one of these and whatever amount you get tells you right away how much of a monthly discount you'll get if you sign your lease today." Of course, every piece had the $10 amount on it. Occupancy went from 91 percent to 100 percent.

Out of the Mouths of Babes

In-store marketing was the only type of marketing that a streetwise dentist could use. Even then he couldn't allow his efforts to be perceived as advertising. Otherwise, there would be serious repercussions.

He had two waiting rooms, one for adults and one for the children. In the kids room he had a free Space Invaders video game for them to play. The kids went nuts. They would go back to school with their new toothbrush, fresh from a fleecing for not flossing. Then, as soon as the Novocain wore off from the five cavities they'd had filled, they'd tell all of their school chums about the free Space Invaders.

Kids were begging their parents to take them to the dentist. But not just any dentist, of course. Begging to go to the dentist? Believe it. And you know how difficult it is to get kids to go to the dentist. It's like . . . pulling teeth!

Just imagine what would happen to his business if he ever installed Pac-Man.

He also used a touch of merchandising around the Christmas season. His tree in the adult waiting room was trimmed with toothbrushes, dental floss, and implements. Nice touch.

There's No Place Like Home

Dorothy found out the hard way that even though the land of Oz and the Emerald City were fascinating places, there's still no place like home. And though the Yellow Brick Road may be far away from Main Street, USA, the principles still apply: There's no place like home . . . or should we say, there's no place like your store or office. That's where you'll find opportunities for increasing sales and for making small improvements on existing successful programs.

5

OFF-PREMISES PROMOTIONS

If you can't bring Mohammed to the mountain, bring the mountain to Mohammed. Now we don't know if Mohammed was a streetfighter or not, but rest assured whoever brought him the mountain was! And the streetfighter's modern-day version of the story is found in the "Off-Premises Promotion."

Essentially, the off-premises promotion is a temporary version of your store or showroom at another location, in either your own city or another city. Over the years we've witnessed successful off-premises promotions executed by art galleries, clothing stores, car dealers, appliance stores, and department stores, just to name a few. We've also seen them held in just about every conceivable location, such as semitrailers on parking lots, county fairground buildings, national guard armories, motel ballrooms, and huge exhibition halls.

The key element is that by going off-premises, you almost automatically create a sense of excitement in the consumer's mind. (It must be a heck of a deal or they wouldn't have gone to the trouble to move all this stuff!")

And it is a lot of trouble. But, properly planned, promoted, and executed, the off-premises promotion can add a nice chunk of change to the bottom line of many retail businesses.

four on the floor

Off-premises promotions fall into four basic categories:

1. General

2. Theme
3. Satellite City
4. Single Dealer

The general and theme type of off-premises promotions are the more widely known. Both of these can offer many advantages to you if you take advantage of the opportunities.

These promotions usually can afford to spend a great deal of money on advertising, which helps in attracting large numbers of people to the shows. Most of these types of shows charge some kind of nominal admission. This has a tendency to qualify most of the consumers because they wouldn't have paid their two or three bucks a head if they weren't remotely interested in the show. (They'll say, "It must be a heck of a deal or they wouldn't be charging admission.")

During these events you'll see a tremendous number of bodies walk by your booth. There is probably little you could afford to do to create as much foot traffic in your own location as you'll get at these shows. But the trick is to turn these lookers into buyers.

The General Show

The general show is classified as such because the participants or exhibitors have nothing in common. Examples are county fairs or half-price shows. In both of these examples, the retail exhibitors can sell just about any type of merchandise. In the case of the county fairs, the consumers are looking for entertainment and not necessarily hard goods. If you deal in a novelty item or food service, you stand a much better chance of selling something than if you came to this fair trying to sell carpeting or washing machines.

But the price of the booths is relatively low compared to what it would cost you in the media to get as many people to see your merchandise firsthand. If you own a restaurant, is there a way you could transport a miniature version of it to this fair? This works especially well if you're dealing with a sandwich or a food that can be eaten with the hands. Dessert items might also be good sellers. The point is that you not only try to make this venture a profit-making one, but you also want to create awareness of your restaurant so that you pick up some new customers.

So, a bounce-back coupon might be in line. They tried you at the fair, but when that fair is over, will they visit your store? To ensure that they do, give them a discount coupon, compliments of the fair. Now you can get them to try you on your home turf. Even so, fitting most retailers into a county fair is not easy. But, it's not impossible.

The half-price fairs or similar promotions can really be valuable. This is usually promoted in conjunction with a radio station, and all the participants are required to provide their merchandise at half the suggested retail. These shows can attract many people, most of whom will be bargain hunters. So you need to load up on a lot of high-profit merchandise that you can unload quickly. The only thing you have in common with all the other exhibitors is that everyone is offering merchandise at half-price.

You really don't have to worry about hurting your regular price credibility at a show like this because the radio station takes all the responsibility of the discount. So it's a good opportunity for you to lower prices and maybe get rid of a lot of stuff that's been on the books awhile.

Service-oriented businesses can take advantage of these types of shows, too. Hair stylists offering half-price haircuts can run a lot of heads through in a short time. Again, provide those bargain hunters with a bounce-back coupon to get them back to your regular location.

If your service business doesn't lend itself to being performed at the show, you can set up a nice display illustrating what you do. Then, once you have their attention, sell gift certificates for fifty cents on the dollar. This would work with car washes, restaurants, oil changes, and so on.

Even though you don't think there's a way for you to make out on these types of shows, at least give it some time and thought. Try to see if there is a way you can take advantage of the program. The cost is usually reasonable and the foot traffic, enormous. But if there's a theme show that pertains to your type of business, that's better yet.

The Theme Show

In theme shows the exhibitors have something in common. Bridal fairs; car shows; sports, vacation, and boat shows; home and energy shows; and business shows all fall into this area.

In each of these examples all the exhibitors have a common thread that appeals to a certain segment of the population. This also means that many of your competitors will be there, so it's vital that you dominate the show and blow your competitor right out of the saddle.

The consumers at the theme shows will be much more qualfied than those attending a general show. They will pay their admission to see specific types of exhibits that they are interested in. They are also more likely to buy, because these shows center around the sale of merchandise, not circus or carnival entertainment. Also, you're not limited to having to offer the merchandise or service at a specific price. It's truly like bringing your store to the people.

So how do you dominate the show? There are a couple of ways. First, there's the use of the premium or free gift. This was done by The Tuxedo Den in Los Angeles when they participated in a bridal fair. It was a perfect off-premises promotion for them because weddings are one of their major profit centers. People attending a bridal fair are probably very interested in weddings. It was a matter of making sure they stopped by The Tuxedo Den's booth, and signed up.

The first thing the store did was have employees standing just inside the front door handing fliers out to the attendees as they walked in. This flier informed the future brides, grooms, and parents-in-law that they would receive a free wine decanter at The Tuxedo Den booth. The response was awesome. People lined up by the tens of dozens to get their free decanter. Of course, in order to receive their decanter they had to fill out a little form that required the bride's name, phone, address, and the date of the wedding. Once they received their free wine decanter, customers were given a free gift certificate good for a free set of matching wine glasses. All they had to do was stop by the store to pick them up. Then, once they got to the store, they were given the opportunity to get an additional six wine glasses and six matching water glasses if they would commit to using The Tuxedo Den for their wedding.

A couple of interesting things are happening here. First, The Tuxedo Den was using free gifts or added values to get the attention of the happy couples. At that time, the competition was offering big discounts on their wedding attire. So to avoid the price war, The Tuxedo Den took the other route. Had everyone been giving away free gifts, they might have considered discounting. But by using free gifts, they automatically protected their regular price credibility and didn't have to worry about developing a discount posture in the mind of the consumer.

Also, by offering the free gifts, they not only wrote a lot of business, but their bottom-line profit margin was much greater than it would have been had they offered the same type of discounts as the competition. Even with giving away the wine decanter to everyone, then the free wine glasses to everyone who stopped in the store, and finally the additional wine glasses and water glasses if they signed a contract, The Tuxedo Den made more actual profit on each wedding then they would have by discounting.

In that three-step giveaway program, notice that they didn't try to sell the wedding at the show itself. They were merely trying, first, to get as many people to the booth as possible. That's the first major problem. Second, they tried to get people to stop in the store. Once the prospects were in the store, sales clerks could spend more time with each prospect and try to close.

And those who didn't stop in the store for their free wine glasses were still included on the mailing list compiled when they received their free wine decanter.

That seems to be the key to success at these types of shows. Don't try to close the big deals at the show. You have thousands of potential buyers walking by. The most important thing is to create as much awareness and impact as you can, while trying to get those prospects back to your store after the show closes so you can spend more time one-on-one to close them.

A similar type of approach was used by a Nautilus club in a sports, vacation, and boat show. Another major health club was going to be there, so the Nautilus club had to figure out a way to dominate the show. The competitor always had one booth with one or two people sitting behind a table asking people to register to win a free membership. They were obviously trying to create a mailing list or telephone calling list, which is a good way to go.

To dominate the show, however, the Nautilus club took their entire club to the show! Every single piece of equipment they had was at the show. That's right, a dozen machines that looked like something out of *Star Wars* were moved to the show.

The promoter of the show was so excited about the idea that he offered to give them four booths for the price of one and to place them right in the center of the arena! They accepted ... and he did!

The show was a week long, which meant that the club had to be closed for a week. To appease the current club members, the Nautilus staff was able, as part of the show agreement, to get free admission tickets to the show for every member of the club. Members could then do their normal workouts, but they had to sign up ahead of time for their specific days and times. Not only did this make the members happy, but it provided the club with a constant demonstration of the equipment, which left the instructors free to talk to the crowd.

Before the show the entire staff had practice sessions. They were taught the exact procedure for handling a prospect, and that procedure was rehearsed. Each staff member was wearing a Nautilus uniform so they were easily identified.

When prospects walked by this massive display, they had to slow down to look. The instructors weren't in the display so much as they were in the aisle watching the crowd. As soon as someone glanced over at the equipment, an instructor would ask, "Are you familiar with Nautilus equipment?" Regardless of the answer, they started to move that person closer to the display to enable them to try one of the machines. While the prospect was doing a few repetitions, the instructor gave a brief sales pitch.

Again, they weren't trying to sell the expensive one-year membership. They were only trying to sell the inexpensive introductory membership at half-off the regular price of $19.50. The prospect would pay on the spot and be scheduled for their first appointment. If they weren't scheduled, they could still register for the drawing to win a free Nautilus sweatsuit. Of course, the registration form required their name, address, and phone number.

Instructors were not to spend more than five minutes with any one prospect. In and out, then go to the next one. In that manner they were able to talk to a tremendous number of people, and get them to not only see but to actually use the equipment (great impact). They made a sales pitch on a very-small-ticket item, then got a name for further follow-up.

What was even more interesting was that this show had two circus acts performing nightly to add to the festivities. A local radio

Congratulations! You have just

Won
ONE FREE VISIT

To All Sports Nautilus Fitness Center
Compliments of the Sports Vacation & Boat Show

Your name was randomly selected from attendees at the Sports Vacation & Boat Show. This prize is non-transferable and must be used before May 25, 1982. Call Jay McClain at 456-1956 to set up your free visit.

Compliments of the Sports Vacation & Boat Show

```
------------------------ COUPON ------------------------
      ALL SPORTS NAUTILUS FITNESS CENTER

                   WINNER
               ONE FREE VISIT
      The bearer of this coupon is entitled to one free visit, by ap-
      pointment only. Cannot be combined with any other discount
      or special. Only one coupon per family.
      Under 18 years must be accompanied by parent.

      Expires 5/25/82
      3602 S. Calhoun                              456-1956
                Across from South Side High School
```

Figure 5-1

station DJ was serving as the emcee for the shows. The manager of the Nautilus club asked the DJ to announce to the people just before the show began that there would be a special demonstration of the Nautilus equipment right after the performance. The DJ did it! Not

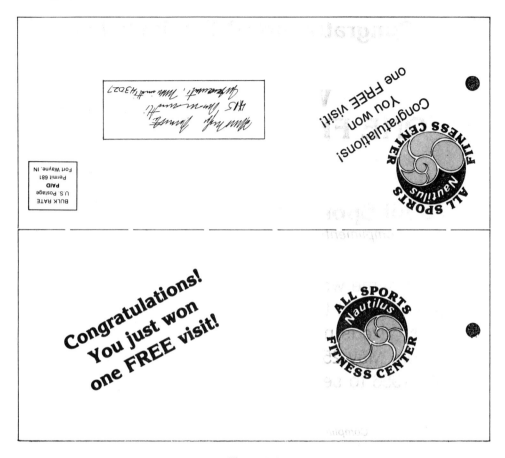

Figure 5-2

only once, but twice every night. And right after each performance there was a flood of interested people at their booth. It didn't cost a penny more to ask for the announcement, and it was probably responsible for an extra 25 percent of people signing up for the free drawing.

Again, the objective was to talk to as many people as possible and get leads for follow-up. Their follow-up was interesting, too. The year before they had just sent out fliers telling everyone that they could still qualify for the introductory discount (see Figures 5-1 and 5-2). This second year, though, they tried a different approach. All instructors were given an equal number of the free-drawing slips. On their own time or while there was some lag time in the club, they were to get on the phone and call each of the people and inform them that they had won a free visit to the club.

For each person who showed up for the free visit, the club employee received a bonus. If they converted that person to a full membership, they would receive a larger bonus. This program was voluntary, but each of the instructors brought in a number of people, which resulted in increased memberships. Since they were using the telephone instead of fliers, there was no cost. No postage or printing to pay. Plus, the personal contact surely made a great deal more impact than a flier would have.

Both the Nautilus club and The Tuxedo Den dominated the show. Each used a little different tactic, but the objective was pretty much the same. First, get them to your booth. Next, get them to your store where you can close them.

The Satellite-City Promotion

This is a little different approach but can be used by a number of retailers. As you've probably gathered by now, off-premises promotions are a lot of work. If things are going well for you, you might not want to bother with them. But if you're looking for a way to boost sales, this can be a good one.

In the satellite-city promotion you're going to take a miniature version of your showroom to another town. It's usually one that's not too far and preferably one that might receive the mass media where you normally advertise. But it doesn't have to be.

If you're located in a large town that's surrounded by a number of smaller ones, this approach might work extremely well for you. First, check your sales slips and see if you're presently getting any business from some of these smaller towns. If you are, see which ones bring you the most business. These towns would be a good starting point to test the program.

For one day, you rent a display area. This could be the ballroom of a hotel in that city or their armory. Using their local media— newspaper and maybe radio—advertise a one-day sale. It means that you have to transport the merchandise to the city and display it. You also have to have some salespeople there to sell the merchandise once the people show up.

Part of the success of the program depends on how efficient the local mass media advertising is. In many cases it's pretty weak. The closer the smaller town is to the larger town, the greater the chance of that local media being worthless, because residents will be influenced more by the larger town's newspaper, radio, and most of all TV.

Direct mail might be a good way to go on this promotion, too. Another alternative is a flier distributed door-to-door by the Boy Scouts or a high school band that wants to make $100 in a couple of hours.

At any rate, these types of promotions do require the use of mass media, which we'll be getting into in greater detail in the chapters to come. The concept is to make it very easy for those people to buy. If they have no outlet in their city for your type of merchandise, this could be an attractive sale to them. There might even be a way to tie it into a local church group or nonprofit organization that will allow you to get them to do all the work for you while you help them raise some money, probably a percentage of the day's sales.

It can also work in reverse. If you're located in a smaller town, you could truck up to the larger one and hold an extravaganza sale.

Either approach is a great way to test the waters to see if you might want to open a location there. If you conduct this promotion in a given city every three months, and each time you blow the doors off, it might indicate a great need for a permanent store there.

The Single-Dealer Promotion

This is by far the most gutsy promotion of the four. With a single-dealer promotion you're putting everything on the line. You pay the media expense, rent the facilities, transport the merchandise and equipment, and provide the personnel. Though it's a high-risk promotion, it can also provide some very high payoffs. It's not recommended that you go into a promotion of this caliber unless you're truly prepared to do it right.

You need a major auditorium, convention center, or coliseum. That in itself will add the magic of the promotion. ("It must be a heck of a sale or they wouldn't have to put it in the Coliseum.")

Next, you don't want to advertise the event too far in advance because as soon as the ads hit it will kill your regular sales. It will also alert your competition as to what you're up to, and they may try a countermove. Even if their countermove, whatever it might be, should be minimally or marginally successful, it still could take some of the excitement away from your promotion. Hush, hush.

You can plan the media buys ahead of time, but don't let the media reps know what the copy is until the ads are to be used. Some reps may try to score points with a client who may just turn out to be one of your major competitors.

You need some good door-busters. A low-ticket item that sells for practically nothing for the first twenty-five people. This is important because when the majority of the crowd gets there, you want to make sure that they see a big crowd. It adds to the excitement. In the case of Classic Stereo, the door-busters were Koss Head Phones for 99 cents (regularly a $45 value). They even sold Sony cassette tapes for 10 cents each.

Your suppliers should be helpful in providing you with this type of giveaway merchandise. Also, try to use co-op advertising funds as much as you can. Try asking your suppliers if they know of any "key city" money lying around somewhere, unused. This is co-op money that hasn't been used by some of the other dealers, so it gets thrown into a special general fund. It's often made available for special events, so it certainly doesn't hurt to ask for it. You might also find some 100 percent co-op money lying around somewhere.

Another area in which your suppliers can be very helpful is in providing the personnel to help sell the merchandise at the show. Sales reps from the various lines are usually excellent retail salespeople and are often willing to help out on a project that can move a large amount of their inventory.

Most of these major lines are displayed at industrial trade shows that the retail merchants attend. Those displays are often very impressive and sometimes can be made available for your show. Again, ask your sales reps if they have a trade show booth that you can use to make the show look that much more impressive.

Close your regular locations a day before the show. This will give you much-needed time to set everything up, plus it makes that show look that much more impressive. ("It must be a heck of a deal or they wouldn't have closed their regular location for a day!")

We've seen the pulling power of a single-dealer show and it can be awesome. People will pay admission to come to your show to buy merchandise. It's a retailer's dream.

Other items to consider might be to rent some of the additional space to a noncompetitive but complementary business. In the case of Classic Stereo, they added a record shop. They rented the space to the record shop and also got a percentage of the take. They might also have worked with a major appliance store that didn't handle much stereo equipment. A computer store might also fit in nicely. It's a good way to cover some of the expenses and to expand the scope of the show and attract more people. In your agreement with these other outfits, try to get them to devote some of their advertising dollars to push the show, but make sure that you get top billing. You don't want to lose the impact of the single-dealer promotion.

Last, you might want to consider setting up a cross-promotion with a popular restaurant in the area as a ticket-to-event cross-promotion (as explained in chapter one). When charging $2 for admission, you can ease the pain by providing them $2 off their next Pizza Hut pizza or whatever you line up. They will often participate if you merely pick up the cost of the printing and paper of the coupons. If you're the one setting it up, you might ask that they promote the event internally for you. Try to get the outside marquee for a week and maybe table tents, danglers, placemats, or tray liners for inside. It's inexpensive advertising for you, and everyone benefits. Off-premises promotions are something you might not want to jump into right away. Especially the single-dealer type, where you have a high degree of risk. But do think about them. See if there is a way you might be able to benefit from this alternative merchandising method. After all, ("It must be a heck of an idea, or we wouldn't have bothered writing this chapter")!

6

Streetsmart
Direct Mail

One person's junk is another's mail. Of course, it's only junk if they don't read it. And most mail advertising doesn't get read, yet enough does so that it can make direct mail advertising a very effective and efficient means of advertising for you.

There's a big difference of direct mail and that of most of the other techniques discussed so far. Direct mail costs money! The trick is to spend as little money as possible while generating the greatest possible return.

Keep in mind that the title of the chapter is "Steetsmart Direct Mail." If you are interested in traditional mass-mailing techniques, there is plenty of material out on the subject. In traditional direct mail, you get a bulk permit number and buy a mailing list from a list broker, or maybe choose your list from the SIC (Standard Industrial Classification) code. These techniques have been around for years.

Streetsmart direct mail is a different story. How do you get someone else to pay for your postage? How can you develop a mailing list of your customers or your competitor's customers? How can you get 12 pieces distributed for the price of one, or better yet 28,000 for the price of 550? How can you share the cost of postage, printing, and production of a mailer a dozen different ways? What of some of the direct mail alternatives that cost nothing to get the message distributed? Sound interesting? It is.

One of the basic rules of streetfighting is to look for the opportunities. In direct mail that means finding ways to get lower costs or free postage. In dealing with the post office, however, you'll soon discover that there is no way you can negotiate a better rate. No matter if you're the most skilled negotiator around, you're not going to get the post office to allow you to mail two for the price of one, or to give you a bonus mailing. You're dealing with a monopoly, and the worst kind at that—a governmental bureaucracy.

In later chapters you'll be learning techniques for negotiating a better price from radio and TV stations. You'll learn how to find out what motivates the person you're dealing with so you can appeal to that motivation, thus allowing you to get what you want. But at the post office you'll find no motivation to appeal to.

In short, you won't find many streetsmart opportunities with the post office. You must look elsewhere to find ways of getting that postage stamp to do more for you.

Stuff It—Free

The first place to look is within your own organization. Ask yourself, "What am I presently mailing out that has nothing to do with advertising?" In many businesses it's the monthly billing of invoices or statements. The postage, you already have to pay for. The envelope, you already have to pay for. So get the most out of it. Put some advertising in those envelopes. That, you won't have to pay for, except for some inexpensive printing.

Advertising to your regular customers is a very good idea. They're easier to sell than a person who has never been to your store. Give them a reason to buy more. If you have a sale coming up, let them know about it with a statement stuffer. If you're introducing a new line of merchandise, let them know with a statement stuffer. If you're running a contest, let them know with a statement stuffer. The cost of distributing that piece of advertising is zero (a streetfighter's favorite price).

Supplier Side

Next, what else is being mailed regularly? Checks to suppliers. You have to pay your bills and mail them to the suppliers, so stuff the same advertising in their return envelopes, too. In both of these examples, you'll get close to 100 percent of those prospects opening the envelopes and at least glancing at your advertising. In most direct mail, you're lucky if 5 percent of the recipients do that.

The point is, the cost is so low you have no excuse for not doing it. So, stuff it.

Selling your regular customers is nice, but let's use the same idea for reaching some new customers. No, it doesn't mean you're going to start billing customers who have never been in your store. But you could stuff your advertising in someone else's statement! Very similar to a cross-promotion, only instead of providing an added value when someone pays at the register, you're providing your merchant partner the opportunity to offer his or her charge customers a little thanks for paying their bills.

Think back to the example in chapter one on cross-promotions. If you really wanted to get technical, what went on between the Nautilus club and the tennis club was actually a form of direct mail. The tennis club mailed out 1,000 coupons to their members along with their regular monthly newsletter.

Twelve of One, Dozen of the Other

A multiunit restaurant operation conducted a direct mail campaign that blew the doors off by allowing them to get twelve discount cards distributed for the price of one. In the original version, the mailing piece was a standard 8½-by-14 inches folded three times. Inside a dozen discount cards were printed on the piece, with the name of the company that received it typed on each card. This was obviously done by an elaborate word processing device. The sheet was perforated to make it easy to separate the cards. These cards were employee discount cards, similar to the discount cards mentioned in the cross-promotion chapter. Each sheet of twelve was mailed to a business in a given area. Recipients were asked to hand them out to their employees as a nice little extra benefit.

When the mailing went out, it literally blew the doors off. The only problem with the program was that it was a little on the expensive side. Not the postage so much, but the company that provided the service was not that cheap. They insisted that their special mailing list and word processing capabilities were the reason for its success.

The Small-Town Small Improvement

To do this same program in a small town of 10,000 or less is cost prohibitive. Thus, the concept was borrowed and adapted. The same basic mailer was used, except no word processing, on an 8½-by-11-inch format. The message told the employers merely to write or type in the name of their business on the twelve cards, then cut them out (it wasn't perforated like the original) and give them to their employees (see Figures 6-1 and 6-2).

The addresses were gathered in a very elaborate way: The waitresses went through the boldface listings in the white pages of the phone book, and hand-addressed the pieces whenever they had slow time. Usually in the afternoon, after their lunch crowd had cleared out. No computer. No word processing. No expensive service charge. But did it work as well? Oddly enough, it worked even better! The only reason we can attribute that to is the same reason cake mixes almost died.

Just Add Water

When cake mixes were first introduced, they fell flat on their Duncan Hines. Nobody bought them. After a bit of motivational research, manufacturers found that housewives felt guilty about using a mix. All they had to do was add water. It was so easy, they had emotional problems dealing with it. To correct the problem, producers made the housewives add one other ingredient. An egg. The rest is history.

Possibly because the cheap version required more involvement on the part of the employer to write or type the name on each card, then cut them out, it worked better. We don't know if that's the reason, but it makes sense to us.

Another advantage was that they were hand-addressed. We got a call from one of the companies. They told us, "It was damned refreshing to get a piece of junk mail that was hand-addressed." Not

Dear Employer,

Here's an exciting employee benefit program that won't cost you a cent!

For the next sixty days, everytime one of your employees visits Pizza Hut, by merely presenting their Discount Card, they'll receive TEN PERCENT OFF the regular menu price of any Pizza Hut food purchase.

The card is then returned to your employee, and may be used over and over for the next two months!

All you have to do is have someone type or write in the name of your business on the cards and distribute them to your employees. If you have more than twelve employees, call us at 749-9584 for additional cards. Do it today! So your employees can get the full benefits of this exciting two month program!

DISCOUNT CARD
The Bearer of this card
is an employee of
_____

and is entitled to a 10% discount off the regular
menu price of any food item at Pizza Hut.
The New Haven Pizza Hut® restaurant
and other participating Northeastern Indiana Pizza Hut restaurants.
Retain this card and use it everytime you visit us through
April 13, 1981.

DISCOUNT CARD
The Bearer of this card
is an employee of
_____

and is entitled to a 10% discount off the regular
menu price of any food item at Pizza Hut.
The New Haven Pizza Hut® restaurant
and other participating Northeastern Indiana Pizza Hut restaurants.
Retain this card and use it everytime you visit us through
April 13, 1981.

DISCOUNT CARD
The Bearer of this card
is an employee of
_____

and is entitled to a 10% discount off the regular
menu price of any food item at Pizza Hut.
The New Haven Pizza Hut® restaurant
and other participating Northeastern Indiana Pizza Hut restaurants.
Retain this card and use it everytime you visit us through
April 13, 1981.

DISCOUNT CARD
The Bearer of this card
is an employee of
_____

and is entitled to a 10% discount off the regular
menu price of any food item at Pizza Hut.
The New Haven Pizza Hut® restaurant
and other participating Northeastern Indiana Pizza Hut restaurants.
Retain this card and use it everytime you visit us through
April 13, 1981.

DISCOUNT CARD
The Bearer of this card
is an employee of
_____

and is entitled to a 10% discount off the regular
menu price of any food item at Pizza Hut.
The New Haven Pizza Hut® restaurant
and other participating Northeastern Indiana Pizza Hut restaurants.
Retain this card and use it everytime you visit us through
April 13, 1981.

DISCOUNT CARD
The Bearer of this card
is an employee of
_____

and is entitled to a 10% discount off the regular
menu price of any food item at Pizza Hut.
The New Haven Pizza Hut® restaurant
and other participating Northeastern Indiana Pizza Hut restaurants.
Retain this card and use it everytime you visit us through
April 13, 1981.

DISCOUNT CARD
The Bearer of this card
is an employee of
_____

and is entitled to a 10% discount off the regular
menu price of any food item at Pizza Hut.
The New Haven Pizza Hut® restaurant
and other participating Northeastern Indiana Pizza Hut restaurants.
Retain this card and use it everytime you visit us through
April 13, 1981.

DISCOUNT CARD
The Bearer of this card
is an employee of
_____

and is entitled to a 10% discount off the regular
menu price of any food item at Pizza Hut.
The New Haven Pizza Hut® restaurant
and other participating Northeastern Indiana Pizza Hut restaurants.
Retain this card and use it everytime you visit us through
April 13, 1981.

DISCOUNT CARD
The Bearer of this card
is an employee of
_____

and is entitled to a 10% discount off the regular
menu price of any food item at Pizza Hut.
The New Haven Pizza Hut® restaurant
and other participating Northeastern Indiana Pizza Hut restaurants.
Retain this card and use it everytime you visit us through
April 13, 1981.

DISCOUNT CARD
The Bearer of this card
is an employee of
_____

and is entitled to a 10% discount off the regular
menu price of any food item at Pizza Hut.
The New Haven Pizza Hut® restaurant
and other participating Northeastern Indiana Pizza Hut restaurants.
Retain this card and use it everytime you visit us through
April 13, 1981.

DISCOUNT CARD
The Bearer of this card
is an employee of
_____

and is entitled to a 10% discount off the regular
menu price of any food item at Pizza Hut.
The New Haven Pizza Hut® restaurant
and other participating Northeastern Indiana Pizza Hut restaurants.
Retain this card and use it everytime you visit us through
April 13, 1981.

DISCOUNT CARD
The Bearer of this card
is an employee of
_____

and is entitled to a 10% discount off the regular
menu price of any food item at Pizza Hut.
The New Haven Pizza Hut® restaurant
and other participating Northeastern Indiana Pizza Hut restaurants.
Retain this card and use it everytime you visit us through
April 13, 1981.

Figure 6-1

Figure 6-2

only that, they asked if they could get a few hundred more coupons for all their employees. We complied.

Striking Out When Bowling for Dollars

For years we tried to get the bowling alleys to do cross-promotions for Pizza Hut. But they refused. They sold their own frozen pizza and they didn't want to lose the business to our client. But bowlers are big pizza eaters and big beer drinkers, so we stuck with it.

Finally, someone suggested that we go through the Bowling League Association. We contacted the director of the association and explained that we wanted to offer their members a 10 percent discount card. She was overjoyed at the opportunity and gave us a list of all the league secretaries along with the number of teams in each league. What happened next was fantastic.

A Perfect Game Plan

We prepared the discount cards as for the employee program but with 6 cards instead of 12. This would allow each team member a card plus a couple of alternates.

Our list consisted of a total of 550 leagues each with between 4 and 12 teams. A cover letter explaining the program was sent to league secretaries from the association director (see Figure 6-3). With the

Bowling Associations of Fort Wayne

MEMO: To All League Secretaries

FROM: Sybil Howe

SUBJECT: Pizza Hut "Ten Pin Discount Cards"

    Enclosed you will find a quantity of Bowler's Discount Cards, good for 10% off the regular menu price of any food item at Pizza Hut.

    These have been secured by our association for all our league members at no cost to us. As you pick up scores from your team captains this week, please give one full sheet to each captain, so they may distribute them to their team members.

    Incidentally, I am still "Secretary" of the Associations, not President as is indicated on the cards. I have enough trouble keeping the Republican and Democrat presidential candidates straight, without getting involved in politics.

Best regards,

Sybil Howe

Sybil Howe
"Still Secretary"

SH/sjh

Figure 6-3

Bowling Associations of Fort Wayne

Sybil Howe
President, Women s and Mixed Leagues

Dear Team Captain,

Through a special arrangement with the Fort Wayne area Pizza Hut restaurants, we have secured for all our bowlers the attached "Ten Pin Discount Card".

The card entitles you to a TEN PERCENT discount off the regular menu price of any food purchased at the participating Pizza Hut restaurants listed on the card.

Distribute the cards as soon as possible so all our members may take advantage of this offer. Also, note that there are *six* cards attached. The extra, or extras are for you to pass along to your favorite substitute. Or in the event of Mixed Leagues, your favorite substitute couple.

Sincerely,

Sybil Howe

SH/ww

Sybil Howe.
President Womens and Mixed Leagues

 TEN PIN DISCOUNT CARD
The Bearer of this card is a member of the
BOWLING ASSOCIATIONS OF FORT WAYNE
and is entitled to a 10% discount on the regular menu price of any food purchased at the following Pizza Hut restaurants:
FORT WAYNE · AUBURN · BLUFFTON · DECATUR · WARSAW · NEW HAVEN
and other participating
Northeastern Indiana Pizza Hut Restaurants
DINE IN OR CARRYOUT   Discount Card Expires April 30. 1980

 TEN PIN DISCOUNT CARD
The Bearer of this card is a member of the
BOWLING ASSOCIATIONS OF FORT WAYNE
and is entitled to a 10% discount on the regular menu price of any food purchased at the following Pizza Hut restaurants:
FORT WAYNE · AUBURN · BLUFFTON · DECATUR · WARSAW · NEW HAVEN
and other participating
Northeastern Indiana Pizza Hut Restaurants
DINE IN OR CARRYOUT   Discount Card Expires April 30. 1980

 TEN PIN DISCOUNT CARD
The Bearer of this card is a member of the
BOWLING ASSOCIATIONS OF FORT WAYNE
and is entitled to a 10% discount on the regular menu price of any food item at the following Pizza Hut restaurants:
FORT WAYNE · AUBURN · BLUFFTON · DECATUR · WARSAW · NEW HAVEN
and other participating
Northeastern Indiana Pizza Hut Restaurants
DINE IN OR CARRYOUT   Discount Card Expires April 30. 1980

 TEN PIN DISCOUNT CARD
The Bearer of this card is a member of the
BOWLING ASSOCIATIONS OF FORT WAYNE
and is entitled to a 10% discount on the regular menu price of any food item at the following Pizza Hut restaurants:
FORT WAYNE · AUBURN · BLUFFTON · DECATUR · WARSAW · NEW HAVEN
and other participating
Northeastern Indiana Pizza Hut Restaurants
DINE IN OR CARRYOUT   Discount Card Expires April 30. 1980

 TEN PIN DISCOUNT CARD
The Bearer of this card is a member of the
BOWLING ASSOCIATIONS OF FORT WAYNE
and is entitled to a 10% discount on the regular menu price of any food item at the following Pizza Hut restaurants:
FORT WAYNE · AUBURN · BLUFFTON · DECATUR · WARSAW · NEW HAVEN
and other participating
Northeastern Indiana Pizza Hut Restaurants
DINE IN OR CARRYOUT   Discount Card Expires April 30. 1980

 TEN PIN DISCOUNT CARD
The Bearer of this card is a member of the
BOWLING ASSOCIATIONS OF FORT WAYNE
and is entitled to a 10% discount on the regular menu price of any food item at the following Pizza Hut restaurants:
FORT WAYNE · AUBURN · BLUFFTON · DECATUR · WARSAW · NEW HAVEN
and other participating
Northeastern Indiana Pizza Hut Restaurants
DINE IN OR CARRYOUT   Discount Card Expires April 30. 1980

Figure 6-4

129

letter was a sheet of cards for each team in the league. On the card was an explanation to the team captain, who was instructed to cut the cards out and pass them out to each of their members (Figure 6-4).

This program was a four-step distribution process. A little complicated, but very interesting. We prepared 550 envelopes containing between 4 and 12 sheets of discount cards. The sheets were given to each of the team captains, who then gave each of their team members a discount card.

The total cost of this direct mail program was under $1,000. This included the labor, postage, printing, and production. It delivered a total of 28,000 discount cards!

The next year the association got a computer and for $24 the list was spit out on mailing labels for us, which saved even more money and time.

Become the Expert

Using a little more of a traditional approach to direct mail can also be useful. But you need a good mailing piece to make it work. Newsletters are such a device. With newsletters you can become the expert in your area. Even though you're a merchant, to get the edge over your competition you need to be in the information business. Teach your customers how to become better consumers. Once they know how to buy quality, and assuming yours is a quality business, you'll be way ahead of all the others.

The more narrowly targeted your customer base is, the more important direct mail, and especially newsletters, is to you. The fabric and yarn company you read about earlier is such an example. When the owner first opened her business, she wanted to advertise on TV, radio, newspapers, and billboards. She was excited about the idea. But we had a problem with that. We reasoned that most of the mass media would be grossly inefficient for her business. Even with the soaps and the so-called "women's" pages in the newspaper, it would not be very easy to target her audience. First, most of her audience would be women. There might be a few exceptions, like Rosy Greer, who does needlepoint, but Rosy didn't get into town very often. So, we assumed an all-female audience. Next, of all women in the area, only about 5 percent sewed. So the target audience was very narrow. With mass media, it would be hard to hit them. We felt that the major portion of her ad budget should be placed in direct mail.

Getting the List

The first problem was coming up with a list. So she had to start by running some mass advertising to announce a grand opening sale to let the public know she was there. Then, when customers came in, each had the opportunity of winning $50 worth of free fabric in a drawing. The entry blank required name, address, and phone (Figure 6-5). Instant mailing list. (See also Figure 6-6.)

She started out with 600 names and over the course of three years built that list to well over 6,000. That list of names is gold to her. Six thousand people who sew, quilt, and needlepoint. You can't get that from an ad in the newspaper, no way.

Once she started getting her list together, she sent out a newsletter. (Figure 6-10). It gave these people patterns and information about sewing and the like. It was also a pretty hard selling piece telling her customers what's going on and what's on sale (see Figure 6-7). Then she always give her readers first crack at sale merchandise. The newsletter was mailed so that readers would find out about the sale a couple of days before the ad was in the newspaper.

Fullerton's
Fabric and Yarn
WASHINGTON SQUARE

FREE DRAWING!

Name ____________________

Address ____________________

City ____________________

State ____________________ Zip ______

Phone ____________________

Figure 6-5

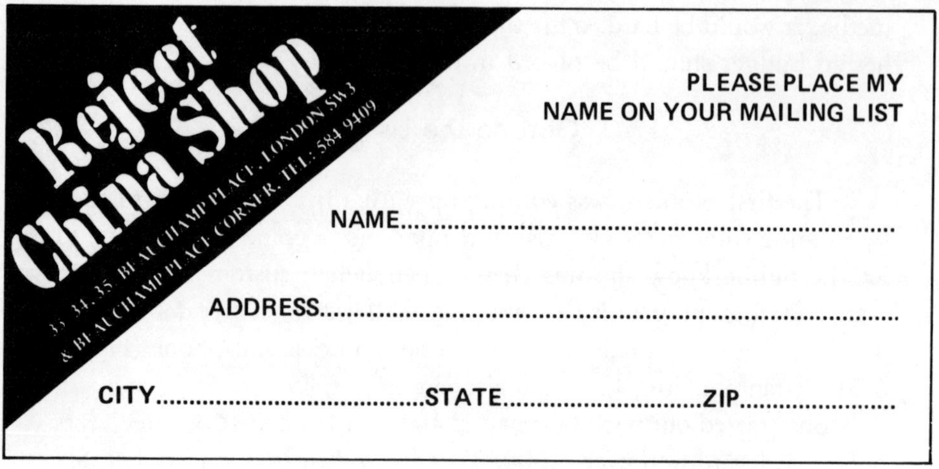
Reject China Shop
33, 34, 35 BEAUCHAMP PLACE, LONDON SW3
& BEAUCHAMP PLACE CORNER. TEL: 584 9409
PLEASE PLACE MY NAME ON YOUR MAILING LIST
NAME
ADDRESS
CITY
STATE
ZIP

Figure 6-6

Because of the urgency of the message, most of the sale items would be sold before the newspaper ad hit. Incidentally, the primary reason for the newspaper ad was to justify the reason for the newsletter readers to buy early. Plus, it would bring in a few new customers who would then get on the mailing list.

Even businesses that appeal to the masses can benefit from a newsletter. Auto repair, health clubs, greenhouses, nightclubs, just about any retail business can benefit. The newsletter allows you to keep in touch with customers. Your customers are open season for a competitor, and it's much cheaper to keep a regular than to find a new customer.

The newsletter can be as simple or elaborate as you like, but if you're just beginning, do yourself a favor, keep it simple. The karate school mails out a newsletter every month (Figure 6-7). It's typewritten and mentions which students have been promoted, new students, and other information about the club. Very simple.

The nightclub uses a newsletter to talk of past promotions and parties. This lets everyone know that if they missed the last party, they missed a good one, and they shouldn't make the same mistake again. Then, of course, the newsletter promotes upcoming events. The letter is written in a fun-to-read style and features a drink-of-the-month—some elaborate concoction the bartenders would come up with. Fun and easy.

PARKER SHELTON
Karate

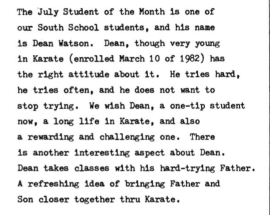

422 W. COLISEUM BLVD. • FORT WAYNE, INDIANA 46805 • 482-2270

JULY NEWSLETTER

The July Student of the Month is one of
our South School students, and his name
is Dean Watson. Dean, though very young
in Karate (enrolled March 10 of 1982) has
the right attitude about it. He tries hard,
he tries often, and he does not want to
stop trying. We wish Dean, a one-tip student
now, a long life in Karate, and also
a rewarding and challenging one. There
is another interesting aspect about Dean.
Dean takes classes with his hard-trying Father.
A refreshing idea of bringing Father and
Son closer together thru Karate.

July Student of the Month
Dean Watson

We would like to welcome our
new members who joined the
North School in June.

Brad Bloom
Laura Shie
Cheryl Favrote
Dave Clayborn
Justin Fredricks
Ray Ernsberger
Chris Mattern
William Bryan

We would like to wish all of our students
who are participating in promotions at
Mr. Yarnell's dojo good luck. These
students will be leaving the North School
at 6:30 a.m. on Saturday, July 31st.
They will be returning to Ft. Wayne as soon
as promotions end.

We want to congratulate those students who
were promoted on July 10 at the North School.
Jerry Lash - 9th Kyu
David Hasty - 9th Kyu
Mark Bower - 9th Kyu
Chuck Holbrook - 9th Kyu
Herb Beltz - 9th Kyu
Saleem Zawawi - 9th Kyu

Figure 6-7

133

20th Century Automotive publishes a newsletter (Figure 6-8 and 6-9). One sheet of paper and written entirely by their own mechanics. It wouldn't necessarily win a Pulitzer prize (who are we to talk), but it does tell the customers important things about their cars, especially self-help items: the difference between the various oil filters, tires, what to check when you pump your own gas, and so on. Very helpful.

There is probably not a business around that couldn't benefit from a newsletter. Accountants and lawyers, stereo dealers, you name it. Many times you'll find that your employees will be very helpful with the writing.

Stay away from "employee-of-the-month" or "customer-of-the-month." Though it's a nice stroke, it's boring to the majority of the readers and will turn them off. Stick with hard news: that is, information you think they will really use. You'll probably get some very good ideas from your own trade publications. Besides, all you need is for your employee-of-the-month to get caught embezzling from you, or your customer-of-the-month to hit the front page of the local paper for molesting a child, and your credibility is shot.

As for the format, again, the simpler the better. One of the easiest and cheapest formats is a single sheet of paper printed on both sides. It can be folded in thirds, stapled, and used as a self-mailer, to save the expense of an envelope. (See Figure 6-10 and 6-11.) Typesetting will cost you more, but makes it easier to read and allows you to get more information on the page. But typewritten can be just as effective. Look at the examples and choose one that's best for you.

If you don't want to get tied down to one a month, try it once and see the reaction. You can do it quarterly or every other month to begin with. Some businesses with a high degree of turnover might want to do it weekly or every other week. It's up to you. You have complete control.

By Invitation Only

After-hours sales or closed-door sales many times can be effective. One of the reasons is that you are allowing the customers to feel that they're very special. These sales are usually done just for your existing customers and, of course, through direct mail.

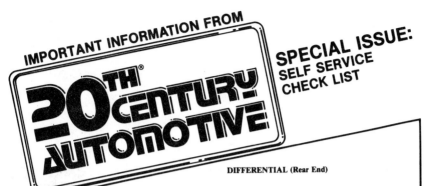

DIFFERENTIAL (Rear End)

Better leave this to your regular service facility. Wherever you have your service done make sure they check the oil level . . . lackadaisical service here can easily cost you $250.00.

AUTOMATIC TRANSMISSION

Check once a month, more frequently if you *know* you have leaks. Instructions are stamped on. the dipstick regarding fluid type, and transmission selector position needed to get an accurate check i.e., Check in park, with fluid hot, on a level surface. Use Dexron II). Dipstick is usually located at the passenger side rear corner, near the firewall.

ENGINE OIL

Check *as often as you can!* When you fill up; once a week; once a day, you can't check it too often. Change interval is *still* 3 mo. — 3000 miles, despite exaggerated claims by the manufacturers of 12 months or 7500 miles; check your owners manual and *READ THE FINE PRINT!* Oil changes and filter changes are the *cheapest insurance* you can buy to guarantee long engine life! By the way, there are devices available that make it possible to check your oil from *inside* your car, for those who like staying dry and warm.

BATTERY WATER

Check once a month. Some new batteries are sealed and cannot be checked. The fluid level should cover the plates. Use tap water to refill . . . studies show that the increased battery life gained by using distilled water averages only 5 days.

BELTS

Check once a month, they should be tight, oil free, and unfrayed. Belt Drive surfaces that are shiny (glazed), or belts that have flipped (rolled over) should be replaced.

HOSES

Should be firm, not hard or soft; they should be kept free of grease or oil (petroleum products eat rubber), and the clamps should be kept tight. Replace at the first sign of cracks or swelling (or every 3-4 years if you want to be real safe).

BRAKE FLUID

The master cylinder is usually located on the firewall, on the driver's side of the car. Some reservoirs are transparent, and some are not. For those which aren't, the lid is secured by a bail, which locks into notches on the master cylinder cap. Fluid requirements are usually stamped into the cap i.e., Use only DOT 3 from a sealed container) CAUTION: Don't spill! Brake fluid takes off paint and eats plastic!

POWER STEERING

Check once a month, the power steering reservoir is located right on the pump (usually on the driver's side of the engine, near the fan). The dipstick is part of the cap, and is marked with hi and low level marks. PLEASE NOTE: Do not use automatic

1001 Leesburg Road • Fort Wayne, Indiana 46808 • Phone 432-5325
"If we can't fix it, it can't be fixed!"

Figure 6-8

135

20TH CENTURY AUTOMOTIVE

CHECK FOR THE FOLLOWING ITEMS

- AUTOMATIC TRANSMISSION
- BATTERY WATER
- BELTS
- BRAKE FLUID
- DIFFERENTIAL (Rear End)
- ENGINE OIL
- HOSES
- POWER STEERING
- RADIATOR
- TIRES

transmission fluid unless it is specifically noted to be acceptable in power steering systems. The pressures in a transmission are ¼ or less of those used in power steering, and some fluids will breakdown and cause damage under the extreme pressures.

RADIATOR

Check once a week. Keep it full of year round (permanent) antifreeze. If you have a closed system you can add at the overflow tank, and it will be drawn into the radiator. Never allow the system to get "muddy" looking, and never open the system while it's hot (you can check for pressure by squeezing the upper radiator hose).

TIRES

Check once a week — maximum inflation pressure (cold) is stamped into the side of the tire, and is the best pressure to use for the best gas mileage and wear. Rotate every 6000 miles (front to rear will do) or every other oil change and you'll double your tire life.

We at 20th Century Automotive have drawn up this sheet as a service to our customers who utilize self service gas stations. We hope it saves you both time and money. If you have any questions on what to do, or where to find something, please stop by and ask, we'll be glad to help. Happy motoring!

Figure 6-9

136

Hemline

PUBLISHED MONTHLY BY FULLERTON'S

VOL. I NO. 4

SPRING!!!

"Pulled Together"--That's the word for Spring Fashion. Skirts are slimmer, with tucks at the waistline and a kick pleat or slit at the center front. Blouses too are slimmer, with simple lines and shoulder emphasis. Pants are slimmer, tapered in toward the ankles. Jackets, too feature longer, clean lines. It all spells a more "pulled together look" with an emphasis on simplicity, and that means easier sewing in less time.

Colors for Spring are lighter shades of the dusties: mauves, lavendars, celery greens and a light shade of yellow called banana. Earth tones are also good, with colors in the stone-to-taupe range. In fabrics, shiny is in. So is sheer, nubby, loopy and linen-y!

SALES!!!

February is birthday month: George Washington's and ours here at Washington Square Shopping Center. Fullerton's will be part of the celebration beginning February 18th. But for our special customers, all our birthday sale prices will all begin "unadvertised" on February 11th! And sales they will be! TWENTY PERCENT OFF our wide selection of designer wall hangings. Perfect for room make overs and lake cottages. TWENTY FIVE PERCENT OFF our Spring Fashion Double Knits, just in from New York. TWENTY PERCENT OFF our popular placemat fabric to give your kitchen an early Spring. And, FIFTY PERCENT OFF our Spinnerin sweater and afghan acrylic yarn, to keep you busy 'til the thaw!

SEWING FOR BRIDES!!!

Springtime spells weddings. And for the unique in bridal fashions, Fullerton's is the place. More Spring fabric suitable for bridal parties, mother of the bride or groom and the bride herself is arriving weekly. And don't forget...Fullerton's offers a 10% for bridal party orders, and we'll also be happy to custom order special fabric for your wedding!

Fullerton's
Fabric and Yarn
Washington Square • One mile north of Northcrest on North Clinton

Figure 6-10

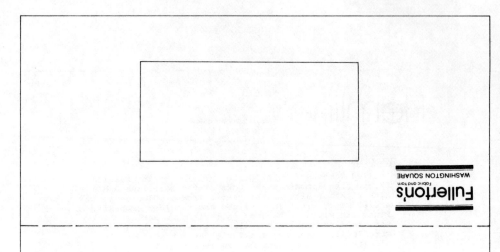

Figure 6-11

Since one of the problems of direct mail is getting people to open the envelope, use an envelope that almost everyone will want to open. An invitation. Printed just like a wedding invitation in the nice half-sized envelopes. Return address on the flap, but no business name. Inside, a beautiful invitation inviting them to your special sale. (See Figure 6-12.) Of course, you'd better come up with a good excuse for the sale.

To expand the list, allow each person to bring a friend. Two for the price of one. Door prizes, refreshments, and you might just have the staff dress up in tuxedos to really make it look special. Have fun with it.

Be sure to address the invitations by hand and, if you really want to get the most out of it, use postage stamps, not a meter or bulk

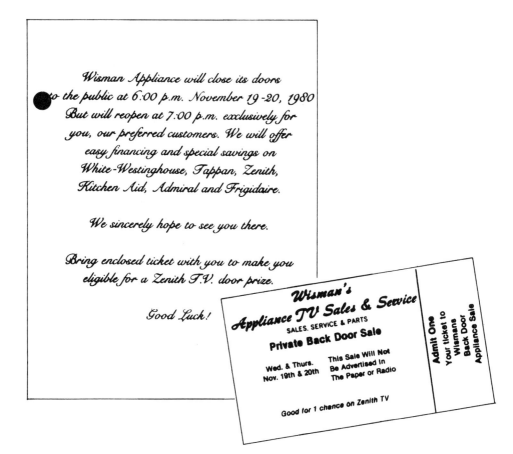

Figure 6-12

permit. First class may be more expensive, but the return should warrant it. You want to give the impression from the appearance of the envelope that they're getting invited to something important. If there is any indication on the outside of the envelope that this is a sale, you'll lose most of them before you get to tell them what a great event this is going to be.

When Wisman's appliance store did this, people who had heard about it but didn't get an invitation begged the doorman to let them in. After a great deal of pondering, one woman who had been let in, and of course didn't want to go home empty-handed, bought something. If you send out invitations, your sale should be more like a party—but one at which the "guests" can buy merchandise.

Pinpoint the Target

Direct mail can be especially good at reaching just a few people. At the Nautilus club, when a member signs up, they receive a card a week later congratulating them on becoming a member. The card also lets them know that they can register other members of their family at a great savings under the family add-on program, if they act soon. Getting a little more from an existing customer.

About three weeks later the club lets them know that if they want to extend their membership an extra 6 to 12 months, now is the time to do it. They will save a great deal by not waiting until the membership expires.

Murray Raphel of Gordon's Alley in Atlantic City, New Jersey, used a very interesting approach to direct mail. His store sells clothes. A detailed mailing list was kept on all customers, including what size they wore in various clothing items. When a number of 41-extra-longs came in, out would go a letter to the 27 people who were 41-extra-long customers to let them know something special in their size had come in. To advertise those items to anyone other than 41-extra-longs, would be a waste. A computer capable of providing this information makes it that much easier.

Covert Compilation

Earlier you read about how to compile a mailing list of your own customers and how valuable that list could be. So what could be one of the worst things that could happen to you? Your competitor getting hold of your list. How could they do it? Here's one possible scenario.

They can sit across from your parking lot and write down the license numbers of all the cars. Those numbers can be converted to a name and address for between 50 cents and $3, depending on the state, and it's done through the State Department of Motor Vehicles or whatever it's called in your area. It's for sale, in most states.

If they want to save some money and just happen to know a police officer on a friendly basis, they may be able to get the same information, free. They'll probably be able to run about three or four a day to play it safe, but it can be done.

This technique is a pain, to be sure, but if your competitor is really aggressive, watch out.

There's an easier way they can do it. Here's how it might happen. Your competitor might approach another retailer with an offer to buy $100 worth of merchandise, high-profit stuff, something the retailer has been trying to get rid of.

Then the friend approaches you with an offer of the opportunity to have a drawing for your customers with the chance to win this $100 item, free to you. The only thing they want from you is for you to mention their name in your advertising for a week and put some posters up in your store. Sounds, great doesn't it? They'll even provide the entry forms and the box for those forms.

If you agree, here's what might happen: You run the drawing, and one of your customers wins the $100 item. The retailer makes a $100 sale of something he probably would have to sell for half that to get rid of, plus a little bit of exposure. And your competitor gets all those entry blanks with the names, addresses, and phone numbers of *your* customers.

Now if your competitor is really smart, he or she will compare those names against the list of his or her own customers. The ones who are going to their store and not yours get nothing. The ones who are going to both might get some kind of coupon. But the ones who are going exclusively to yours and not theirs would get some kind of extremely high-liability discount, such as a free item, just to get them into the store for the first time. And on their mailing list. Ouch!

Third-Class Togetherness

Multimailings are becoming more and more available. Tri-Mark and Val Pak are a couple of companies that come to mind, but there are surely many more. These are companies that put a dozen or more businesses in the same envelope and provide a mass mailing. They can save you 50 percent or better than if you did the mailing yourself, plus they generally get a little better response than does a single mailing. This might be because if a person sees your mailer and isn't interested in your product at that time, into the wastebasket it goes. But when people receive a couple dozen pieces in the envelope, there is bound to be something in there of interest, and you get a short-term stay of execution.

These companies will sometimes negotiate. If you find that the price is firm, then negotiate top position if it's available, or possibly a second color free.

Forming your own cooperative mailing group could be a great value to all participating parties. If you're a business serving other businesses—office furniture for example—you could team up with a printer, computer store, telecommunications company, uniform rental place, window cleaner, commercial real estate agent, restaurants that cater to business lunches, car rental or leasing agencies, and office supplies company, to name a few. All of these merchants need to reach the same target audience—other businesses. By putting you all together in one large envelope, each getting a page, you could cut your mailing costs tremendously and make a big impact at the same time. The obvious one to put the program together is the printer, because they get the printing business from the project. But even so, if just three or four such businesses teamed up, you could save two to three times on a mass mailing.

Another example is the wedding business. Bridal shops, tuxedo shops, florists, caterers, photographers, bands, jewelers, gift shops, and so forth. A group mailing to all the prospective brides could be very effective and the cost cut a dozen or more ways. Again, get your printer to set this one up, after all, who's going to get to do the invitations?

On the Shelf

Direct mail can also be used in emergency situations. What would happen if all of a sudden you had a bad week? You need to do something to boost sales in a hurry, but it would take at least a week or two to get out a mailer with a coupon. By then sales could be even worse.

You can make a small improvement in the disclaimer on your coupons that will give your direct mail pieces unlimited shelf life. Instead of an expiration date, you can put, "Offer expires 30 days from receipt of coupon." Sure there might be some abuse of this expiration date, but the benefits far outweigh the problems.

You can now have your mailing pieces printed, with mailing labels affixed, on the shelf and ready to go when that first snow storm or heat wave hits. When you need them, just take them to the post office. They'll be out weeks sooner than you could have done it otherwise.

Door Hangers and the Telephone—the Mailing Alternatives

Door hangers and your telephone can allow you some alternative ways to reach people with your advertising message at a cost far less than direct mail. At the same time, both of the approaches have some of the same benefits as direct mail.

Print door hangers two or three to a sheet of card stock. Some quick printers may have a die that will cut a hole at the top so the cards are easily attached to a door. If not, have them drill a ⅜-inch hole at the top. Use rubber bands to attach the hanger to the door.

The distribution can be handled in a couple of ways. First, you could approach a nonprofit youth organization, such as the Boy Scouts. Offer to pay them a nickel for each card they deliver. That drops your postage quite a bit right there. You could also go to a local junior high school and ask the principal to suggest a few trustworthy students who would like the job. Instead of paying them on the number of pieces delivered, you could pay them on the number of coupons redeemed. This will ensure that they deliver the amount they were supposed to.

Door hangers are very effective when you need to get your advertising out in a big hurry. When you mail bulk rate throught the post office, it can be up to ten days before delivery. But with door hangers on the shelf, using the "30 days from receipt of coupon" disclaimer, you could actually have your coupons in the hands of consumers in 24 hours.

When you compile your mailing list, you should be getting phone numbers as well. Telemarketing is fast becoming a very big area. To start out, try something very simple and very inexpensive. The phone is already in your store. As it stands now, you're not charged for local calls. This may change in the future, but for now it stands. When your salespeople, clerks, counter people, or any employees, for that matter, are sitting around doing nothing, just waiting for a customer to come in, they could be on the phone drumming up business.

It works like this: Let's say you have a sale coming up in a week. To advertise that sale you're going to mail a circular to your customer list—a traditional approach, but often very effective. During the slow times your salespeople are then required to call people from that list. All they need to do is, first, introduce themselves. Then tell customers that you're having the sale next week and that they should expect to get your circular in the mail soon. Thank them and say, "I'm looking forward to seeing you." That's all there is to it. It will create a greater awareness for the sale. It adds a personal touch. And it costs nothing.

To put a little fire under your people, you could make a contest out of it. This is a small improvement on the technique used by the Nautilus club (Chapter five).

When your employee calls and—provided you have some kind of coupon in the circular, newspaper ad, or whatever—tells the prospect to put the salesperson's initials on the upper left-hand corner of the coupon; it's good for an additional 10 percent off that item. If there is no coupon the initials can go on a certain part of the ad. The employee with the most redemptions, or the highest total sales from those customers redeeming the coupons, wins.

It would be very interesting to track the results. If you were able to reach half of the list by phone, see if the percentage of responses from that half of the list is higher than the half without the phone support.

Eventually you may want to develop a more sophisticated and organized telemarketing program, but for now, use some of that wasted time and a free line and see what can be done.

You Can't Fight City Hall or the Post Office

As far as mass mailings go, we can only tell you from personal experience. Though we firmly believe that direct mail is and will be one of the top forms of advertising, we have a bad taste in our mouth from one little incident.

When the Retail Marketing Institute was first formed, we conducted our first seminar in Lexington, Kentucky. Ten thousand direct mail pieces went out to retailers in and around Lexington. Well, not exactly. We were never sure that all of them made it.

We took our pieces to the post office to drop them off. We didn't want them to get out for two weeks because it would have been too early to have the desired effect. The post office attendant in the bulk mail department told us there would be no problem leaving them there, and we knew there was no chance of their getting mailed accidentally. We had no money in our account at the post office to cover the postage, and they never mail unless you pay up front.

Somehow, though, they were mailed. And the response to the mailing was horrendous. Then the post office called and demanded that we give them a check immediately. Our attorney was quick on the scene, not only refusing to pay for this worthless mailing, but demanding that we get a free one to make up for their blunder.

We should live so long. The local postmaster threatened to get the FBI on us and prosecute us. It didn't take us long to figure out how big a heart the post office has. Even if we could have won the battle, it would have cost us far more than we would have won, so like the typical entrepreneur up against the wrath of the United States government, we conceded. They had our check the next day. And thus began our long love affair with the post office. You can't live with them and you can't live without them.

7

RADIO:
RED-HOT OR RIP-OFF?

"Radio Advertising Is Red-Hot," according to a recent campaign by the Radio Advertising Bureau. We couldn't agree with them more, because if you're not careful—you'll get burned! That's not to say that radio advertising is bad. It's probably the most effective and flexible advertising mass media in your local marketplace. But you have to approach it with a new attitude, a streetfighter's mentality, to make it work.

It used to be that you could buy one spot a day for a year and get some action from it; no more. It's a whole new ballgame with a completely different set of rules. The game's a little more physical these days and it takes a lot more strategy and planning. You have to know the new rules, and how to bend and even break some of those rules, if you want to stay in the running.

The Tarnished Age of Radio

Most books on advertising love to reminisce about the "Golden Age" of radio ... a time when families used to sit around the old radio and listen to "Fibber McGee and Molly," or find out what "The Shadow" knew. The problem is that most retailers today buy radio time the way they did when they used to tune into Walter Winchell every Sunday night at eight o'clock. We hate to burst your bubble, but Walter "ain't on the air no more." Radio is still useful, but not as productive as it once was. The glow is gone and it has slipped into a new era—the "tarnished" age of radio.

Even though radio advertising has lost much of its luster, there's still life left in those rusting transmitter towers and decaying rating books. (Of course, we refer to the rusting towers figuratively, because most stations have the highest quality state-of-the-art electronic equipment. Unfortunately, it does nothing for those decaying rating books, which we regard in the literal sense.)

In all fairness, radio advertising does have some unique advantages over the other mass media. So, first you'll learn about those unique qualities of running a radio campaign, and then we'll rip it a new way to walk. At that point, we'll show you how a streetfighter gets radio to stand on its own two feet.

Even though it's a mass media and will reach listeners throughout your city and beyond, radio is able to narrow the audience and target a specific group of people better than any other of the mass advertising media. This demographic control allows you to target by age and sex, because radio stations program by "format." The format is the station's "personality" and is determined primarily by the type of music they play. Their news department, announcers, DJs, and even the promotions they run also help to make up the personality of the station.

A country/western format will attract a different group of people from those who appreciate a beautiful-music format or a rock format. Even in cities that have four or five "rockers," you'll find that each attracts a little different group. One may have more women than men, while another may scale a little older or younger. Certain products seem to sell better with specific formats. A stereo dealer would probably do better on a rock station, while a western-wear shop should see more results from a country format. A Cadillac dealership should find most of its potential customers tuned into a beautiful-music station, unless they're located in the affluent parts of the rural midwest. Then you may wish to use a country station to attract the "Mercedes and Manure" crowd. Knowing your marketplace is very important in determining your real target audience.

The structure of a radio station is such that it allows flexibility in advertising your products and services. For example, an air conditioning business can have a standing order with a radio station during the summer months to run their commercials only when the temperature hits a particularly high level. This allows the client to advertise at the exact time the product is most needed. As a rule, no other mass medium can react that fast.

Radio stations can broadcast live from your store, and they can give away merchandise on the air, which adds excitement to and awareness of your business. Many times you can get free mentions by providing the station with your products.

Trading and bartering air time for merchandise seems to be a favorite pastime for many radio stations. Dollar for dollar you can come out way ahead when you exchange high-profit merchandise for advertising that you would have to pay the regular rate-card rate for.

Production is cheap. You can have the station produce a spot for you free. But even if you want to have a high-quality radio spot made professionally, the cost may be a fraction of what it costs to do a TV spot.

Right now you're probably saying to yourself that radio seems like a pretty good deal. And it very well can be, but there are many wasted dollars. Don't expect that if you use radio all you'll need to do next is charter a Brink's truck to haul all your money to the bank every day. The fact of the matter is, most radio advertising doesn't work as well as it once did. Many users are beginning to question if they are receiving a decent return on their investment. Merchants aren't seeing the results they got forty years ago, or four years ago for that matter.

One problem is that the cost has gone up and continues to do so. The Radio Advertising Bureau claims that radio rates have risen less than TV or newspaper. It may be so, yet the cost increases are way beyond inflationary levels. In addition to that, their audiences are beginning to dwindle. So, in effect, you are paying more for a smaller, nonattentive audience.

A number of factors are responsible for the dilution of major audiences. For one, there are just more stations to choose from, and with recent deregulation from the FCC, the problem will get much worse before it gets better.

Not only is the audience being fractionalized into more segments, but many radio listeners are turning to nonradio entertainment such as cassette tape players, both in the car and in the hand. Case in point is the increased popularity of the Sony Walkman tape player. CB radios pose another threat to the decaying radio audience, and that's one problem radio stations won't be able to get a handle on. Even in-home listening is being challenged by cable TV's MTV, a video version of a radio station that is capturing many viewers nationwide.

But the biggest danger to the effectiveness of radio advertising is that once you finally reach an audience, those that are tuned in actually may be mentally tuned out.

Is Anybody Really Listening?

Most people listen to radio when they are driving to and from work. The industry refers to this as "drive time." (And you thought we cornered the market on creativity.) The car has played an important role in the success of radio advertising since television usurped most of the big money. The radio in your car is very different from the radio in your home or office because it has push buttons. Five little magic buttons that allow you to change stations. This habit seems to begin in puberty and manifests itself most obviously in the middle to late teens.

Watch a teenager in a car sometime. The first thing they do is start pushing buttons until they find a song that they like. As soon as that song is about to end, usually about the last four bars, they start pushing buttons again for another song. No commercials are heard. Woody has three teenage sons and swears that they can go for months without hearing one radio commercial.

There are those who do hear the commercials. However, unless they hear a commercial over and over again, there is little chance of their remembering it. Because there are so many commercials on the radio, listeners not only try to tune them out physically by button pushing, but they tune them out mentally as well. That means that to have an impact on the listener, an advertiser must place many commercials in a short time span. Increased frequency means increased costs.

Then there are the stations that have taken a completely different approach. To avoid the "commercial clutter," they have started programming "commercial-free" radio in an effort to increase their ratings. It's a last-ditch effort to save themselves, but one that could eventually lead to total ineffectiveness. A wise man once said, "A drowning man will grab at razor blades." These commercial-free blades are aimed right at the stations' wrists.

The commercial-free strategy causes a number of problems. The most disturbing is that they are conditioning the listener to believe that commercials are bad and should not be listened to. By promoting the commercial-free concept, they are in effect conditioning the audience to change the station as soon as the commercial-free segment is over. As an advertiser, you are charged directly as a result of the ratings. But even though a station may have terrific ratings, and many people listen to their music and news, how many of them are actually listening to your commercials?

Many stations will reduce their inventory, that is, the total number of minutes that are available to sell to advertisers. This is often done in conjunction with programming commercial-free segments. With this artificially reduced inventory, the cost per spot goes up. We don't know which is worse, commercial clutter or higher spot prices. But one thing's for sure, radio doesn't work as well as it used to. Reducing the inventory makes it much easier to sell out the station. Sales reps love to tell all their advertisers, "We're all sold out this week." It gives the illusion that the station must really be working because every single available spot has been bought. Then they try to get you to buy earlier and be thankful that you could buy *some* time even though it's costing twice what it should. We never really understood why people who make their living selling radio time would be thrilled to say they have none to sell this week. With nothing to sell, how do they make any money?

We have toyed with the idea of buying our own radio station if this book sells well, and programming it "music free." Nothing but commercials. It may not have a large audience, but those who do tune in sure would be excellent consumers.

There are many problems with radio, as we have just pointed out. Whether it be too many commercials, not enough commercials, or no commercials at all. Their audiences are fickle—jumping from one station to another faster than a flea on a scratching hound. But still their rates continue to rise. That doesn't mean we should raise the white flag. We have not yet begun to fight—streetfight, that is.

You Can't Be Too Rich or Too Repetitive

So, how do we make radio advertising work for you? First you must understand what makes consumers react to advertising. One thing that helps make advertising effective is frequency. Your commercial message must hit the consumer over the head repeatedly before it will begin to make an impact. (We don't mean to sound sadistic, but it works.)

People are constantly bombarded with advertising messages. Studies indicate that consumers are exposed to anywhere from 500 to 1,700 commercial messages every day. From the moment you wake up in the morning and put on your Fruit of the Looms, or cross your heart with Playtex, until you go to bed at night, setting your GE alarm clock as you retire on your Serta Perfect Sleeper, you are constantly barraged with advertising messages.

Your brain can't remember all of these. If it did, you'd have to re-do your bedroom with rubber wallpaper. So to protect your sanity, your brain tunes out most advertising much as Mr. Coffee filters the grounds from what you drink. The majority of advertising ends up just like those coffee grounds—cast away with the morning's leftover scrambled eggs and burnt toast.

One way to break through that filter system in the brains of potential customers is by repetition. You tell your message over and over and over again; and then do it some more. If 3,000 people hear your ad one time, it's worthless. If 2,000 people hear your ad twice, it's semiworthless. But, if the same 1,000 people hear your ad three times or more, it will begin to penetrate that filter system and make an impact. We're not so concerned with how many different people we can reach with our commercial, but rather with how many people we can reach a multitude of times.

One mistake advertisers often make, especially those on very limited budgets, is that they want their ad money to last. They spread their budget over a long period of time, and the commercials are spread throughout the month. Oddly enough, many of those same merchants may think nothing of spending twice that amount on a full-page newspaper ad that will last for one day.

Think of radio advertising as a special boxing match. Your objective is to knock out your opponent, but you're only allowed to throw 30 punches during the entire fight. You'd be better off throwing all 30 punches in one round instead of two punches a round for 15 rounds. By concentrating your effort all at once, you'll begin to make an impact, leaving your opponent little time to recover from the last punch before he gets his once again. Here's a good rule of thumb to follow: If you can't afford to be on strong, don't advertise. Wait until you can afford to be on strong.

On a limited budget, you should concentrate those commercials so that you can reach the same people over and over again. Stations would much rather place your spots so they're spread out over a longer period of time. It's easier for them to schedule that way. But you want to take those 30 commercials that you normally would place during the course of a month and squeeze them into *three days*. You won't reach as many people, but you'll have a greater impact on the ones you do reach.

Another way to increase frequency of the same listeners is to concentrate your spots in the same time of day or "daypart." The audience that is listening in the morning drive time daypart will be different from those listening in the afternoon or evening. There will be some duplication from daypart to daypart, but by and large, you'll find that the same people tune in at about the same time every day. So instead of spreading your spots throughout the day for one week, place them in only one daypart. If people start to complain that they're sick and tired of hearing your commercial, you'll know you're on the right track.

30s vs. 60s

In radio, the cost of 30-second commercials is usually 20 to 30 percent cheaper than 60-second spots. Even though the 60s may be a better deal as far as the cost per second, you are better off using 30s if possible, so that with the same money you can increase your frequency. The key is to ask yourself, "Can I tell my story in 30 seconds?"

Own the Station

We also suggest that you dominate a single station. If you spread your dollars over two or three stations, you will lose much of the effective frequency. Also, the more you spend on any one station the more leverage you'll have with that sales rep to get lower prices and better positions.

If you're worried about not reaching a large portion of your target audience if you buy only one station, relax. You'll be able to overpower those loyal listeners. As for listeners who seem to jump around from station to station like a chicken with its head cut off, here's a comforting thought. Do you know how difficult it is to shoot a chicken with a machine gun from a helicopter? We never gave it much thought either, until Jeff's roommate in school, a Viet Nam vet, shared this heart-warming story with us. There's a real art to it. You see, you don't even try to shoot directly at the chicken, because once you start shooting, the chicken runs around so spasmodically that it's practically impossible to hit it. You simply continue to shoot in the same spot. The chicken will eventually run right into the line of fire. Add a few matzo balls and you're all set.

Your advertising works much like a machine gun. The loyal listeners are goats or sheep—no bouncing around, and easy to hit. But there are a fair amount of chickens out there, and eventually they'll run right into your line of fire too. And what of Jeff's roommate? He now heads up a county SWAT team in the midwest. We just pray that we aren't taken hostage by a band of wild chickens!

The Enemy

Now that we have a good idea of how to place the spots, the next step is to deal with the representatives from the radio station to find out how much all of this is going to cost. They come under a variety of titles such as "sales rep," "salesperson," "radio consultant," and the ever-popular "account executive." Don't let these impressive names throw you, for you have but one rule to remember about the sales force of local radio stations and all peddlers of local advertising for that matter: The media are the enemy.

We need to clarify that point. We are specifically referring to the salespeople of retail advertising on a local level. Any person who wants you to spend your money on their medium is your enemy. Whether it's a TV salesman, newspaper saleswoman, billboard sales representative, Yellow Pages vulture, or even the innocent little high-school cheerleader with an ad to sell you in her yearbook, always remember: The media are the enemy. That's not to say that the minute your sales representative pulls up in your parking lot you immediately run outside and toss a Molotov cocktail in the back seat of his car. We must meet this enemy, not with resistance, but with cunning, so that we capture all the spoils, yet the enemy leaves thinking they won. You must gain this enemy's confidence, get him on your side. As we mentioned in the preface, one of our favorite streetfighting philosophies comes from the movie, *The Godfather, Part II*. At one point in the movie Michael says, "My father once told me, keep your friends close, but your enemies closer."

That's how we learned how to get the most from these media people. We befriended them. We found out their true powers and weaknesses, their motivations and limitations. We learned their business from their point of view. What did we learn? We learned that their job is to sell you their product. If you buy, they make a commission. If you don't, they make nothing. Their first obligation is to sell you—to perform a cashectomy. That's not to say they're bad people. In fact, they're usually very nice. They'll get you tickets to games and concerts or take you to lunch. But their sole purpose in life is to sell you advertising time or space. That's fine and that's fair. But, by understanding their motivation, you can be in a better position to manipulate that person so that you can get what you want, too.

Selling the Sales Rep

Most prices for radio time are negotiable. That's a given fact. Most advertisers buy radio time the way they buy a used car. However, that's backwards. So to avoid picking up a lemon, pay attention.

A station rep will come to your store with a "package offer." Let's say he wants to sell you 25 spots for $1,000. You know you can dicker over the price, so you offer $750 for the 25 spots. If he feels that he will lose the buy unless he rolls with the punches, he'll counter with $950. You make another counteroffer of $800. He counters with $925. You counter. He counters. You counter . . . it sounds more like a scene from *Rocky*. And after you've beaten each other to death, you agree on 25 spots for $900. Sound familiar?

Now let's look at that transaction from a salesperson's point of view. When he walked through your front door, what dollar amount was on his mind? $1,000? No! He's thinking of the commission he'll make if you buy. He's only concerned about what ends up in his pocket. Let's say a sales rep's on 10 percent commission. In the last encounter, the rep had $100 in mind. When you countered with an offer of $750, you took $25 out of his pocket. Naturally, he'll be reluctant to lower the price. Keep in mind that he's not selling a product, but an intangible commodity—time. Once that 30-second time period has passed by, there's no way for the station to sell it again.

To turn this situation around, establish your budget figure up front. If you want to spend $900, let the sales rep know it. As soon as you mention the $900 figure, a little calculator in the back of his mind starts computing his commission. You can almost see the buzzers and bells go off in their heads. He knows he will make $90 if you buy. For your $900, he might come to you with a schedule of 22 spots. You don't negotiate the price of that schedule, but rather the number of commercials you get and where they are placed during the day. Counteroffer with 35 spots for the $900. He'll stary crying about how impossible it would be to get it approved by his sales manager. So, come down to 33 spots and hold firm. Tell him that if he could just sneak this buy through, he has a deal. Now the salesperson must return to the station and use all his years of sales experience and expertise to convince his boss that you must have 33 spots for $900. You've turned *their* sales rep into *your* sales rep.

The station reps don't really care how many spots you get because their commission is based on gross sales. They'd probably throw in the transmitter if they thought they could get away with it. It may not work all the time, but it sure can help you get the most for your advertising dollar.

One interesting negotiating tactic was used by a greenhouse manager when he realized that he ordered 30-second spots but his preproduced commercials were 60s. He asked the sales rep to stop by to see him at the greenhouse. He explained that he'd made a terrible mistake in that he just couldn't afford 60s, nor could he afford to give up the frequency he had already ordered. He then asked very nicely if she would see if it would be possible to change the 30s to 60s, free. Next he handed her a dozen roses, apologized for the oversight, and said that anything she could do to help him would be greatly appreciated. He got the 60s!

You can get a lot more than additional spots or longer commercials for your money, too. Another point of negotiation might be better time slots. Many times a sales rep will come to you with a special package that has a fixed number of spots and costs. In that instance, you can request that the commercials be placed in all drive time. It certainly doesn't cost anything to ask.

Another little trick, after you've gotten just about everything you think you can get, is to ask for matching overnights. These are spots that fall between midnight and 6:00 A.M. Some stations will charge an additional 10 percent for this, but often you can get it thrown in as the final determiner for your name on the dotted line. That means that if you bought 33 spots, overnight you would be able to get an additional matching 33 spots. Granted, not too many people will be listening to the station then, but for free, what could it hurt?

If you get them to throw in the overnights, your last little bit of maneuvering is to get them to bracket those overnights between 5:00 A.M. and 6:00 A.M. This is the hour before the beginning of morning drive time. Out of all the hours in the overnight period, you're likely to pick up the most from this time period. We did that once in a city near the Indiana/Ohio line. There was a time change between the two states, so all of those people in Ohio were actually reached during their drive time.

The Carte Blanche Approach

On a couple of different occasions, we needed to use radio advertising early in the week—on Monday and Tuesday only. Most advertisers request that their spots fall from Wednesday through Friday or Saturday. As a result of this practice, stations are more likely to be sold out later in the week. Some even charge a premium if they can't spread your spots throughout the week. That also means that they must have a lot of unused air time on Monday and Tuesday.

We started talking with the sales manager and he was boasting about how they were sold out toward the end of the following week. We knew that most of the time early in the week was going to be wasted, so we told him that we would buy every available spot for half of what we normally paid. We knew that they wouldn't play more than one of our spots in each commercial break; but still, it could amount to a fair amount of money.

He was very tempted, to say the least, and made a counteroffer of 75 percent of what we normally would pay. We agreed on the condition that he limit it to one spot per hour between 6:00 A.M. and 7:00 P.M. He agreed.

That's exactly the number of commercials we were going to buy anyway. Yet, because of our approach, we were able to save 25 percent. The station was thrilled to death because they thought they were unloading time that was going to be wasted.

That particular approach can really be effective when you know the station is going to eat their inventory. It helps to make the offers so that the spots will air very soon. By then, the station knows if that time has been sold out or not.

Buying early in the week is a very strong negotiation position if you are the type of outfit that does much of its business at that time. We represented a legal clinic that handles many divorces and bankruptcies. They informed us that most of their clients came to them early in the week. It turned out that couples do most of their fighting on the weekend, and by the time Monday rolls around, they are ready to file for a divorce. Bankruptcies seem to work the same way. If an individual in business had a bad week, by Monday they are really ready to bail out.

Knowing this, we were able to approach the radio stations with the "Carte Blanche" technique. It's really attractive to a sales manager to be able to sell all of their unused inventory, even at a greatly reduced rate. The frequency was deadening. The listeners may have gotten sick of hearing those commercials so many times, but the advertisers showed a very healthy return.

The Knee-to-the-Groin Trick

When you have been working with individual sales reps for a period of time, they sometimes get a little cocky. This is especially true for a station rep who knows that his or her station has the best numbers at the best price for your particular audience. They may not be good for any other group, so they become a real pain in the asking price. When they've got you where they want you, it's time to take action and a swift kick in the behind is just not enough.

We ran up against this while working with a stereo dealer. The target audience was men age 18 to 34. One station in town didn't have a great overall audience, but they had a hell of a lot of men 18 to 34.

Since they had little else except inventory, they were by far the best buy in town.

Their sales rep came in one day with his schedule and the prices were substantially higher than what we had been paying. He then drew us a cost comparison between his station and all the others based on the target audience of 18-to-34-year-old men, and they were still the best buy in town, even at that inflated price. We bought the schedule and the rep went back to the station, probably telling everyone how brilliant he was in getting more money out of us.

On his next visit to our office he was all smiles as he carefully laid his proposal on the desk. We then informed him that we had made a change in our marketing strategy and our client was now in an all-out effort to reach *women* 18 to 34. A whole new market that's virtually untapped in the stereo business. His station was one of the worst in that target audience.

As you can imagine, his jaw dropped as low as where our knee was ready to strike. Being an aggressive salesperson, he was immediately on the phone to his sales manager. In about fifteen minutes we were able to come up with a special deal at a spot cost that was lower than what we had originally paid. Of course, the client had no intention of going after the female stereo buyer, but the radio rep didn't know that. Sometimes you have to play games with these people if you want to spend less money. Get inside their minds before you get into your pockets.

Who's Really Number One?

Speaking of games radio people play—how about the ratings game? This is how it works. The new radio rating book comes out. Those stations that do well are very aggressive in promoting that fact. Those that do not do so well are aggressive in promoting the margin of error in the rating system. But for the most part, the stations live and die by the ratings. That's their most important tool in selling their station to you. Isn't it funny that every station seems to claim they're number one? It's very possible that every station *is* number one; odd, but true. They might be number one for left-handed Armenian midgets who listen on Sunday between 7:00 P.M. and midnight, but they are a number-one station, none-the-less.

As soon as the rating book is out, they may send you a flier or brochure proclaiming, "We're number one!" Then right at the bottom in type so small that it almost takes an electron microscope to read it, they'll qualify their proclamation with something like: "Number one for reaching boys entering puberty who listen on Wednesday or during lunch hour."

We admit that our examples may seem a little ridiculous. But, in actuality, though the statistics used by many stations may sound good, they are just as ridiculous as our examples. It was once said that sales reps use rating books much like a drunk uses a lamp post—more for support than illumination.

Remedial Rating-Reading 101

There are people who devote their entire lives to understanding and analyzing the ratings. It's very difficult and complicated. But with a streetfighter's basic understanding of the ratings, you'll be able to sort the good from the garbage.

The only two numbers you need to know are the cost you're paying for a spot and the total number of your target audience listening at a given point. This audience-level figure is called the "average quarter hour." With these two figures, you can very simply compute how much you are paying to reach 1,000 people. This is referred to as "cost per thousand" and is abbreviated CPM. With the CPM you can compare stations like apples to apples and avoid the rotten ones. So if a station rep starts showing you all the tens of thousands of people you can reach with their station, don't get excited. Once you know how much it's going to cost per thousand, you'll know if it's really a good deal or not.

For example, if station WRIP has 1,000 men 18 to 34 listening in the morning drive with a spot cost of $25, the CPM is $25. If station, WJRK reaches 2,000 men 18 to 34 and charges $60 per spot, their CPM is $30. So, even though WJRK has twice as many of your target audience, WRIP is a better buy because their CPM is $5 lower.

Station reps will figure all this for you, but you must make sure they all play by the same rules. In most markets, Arbitron is the standard radio rating service. Surveys are taken once, twice, or several times a year, depending on the size of the market. Some stations do better in one survey than they do in others. But as a general rule, request that all stations submit data from the most recent survey.

Also, radio surveys give two sets of audience figures. One is for the Metro Survey Area, which is usually the county where the station is located and a few surrounding counties, and one is for the Total Survey Area. (This might be as many as 15 to 20 counties.) Generally, the big stations want to use Total Survey Area numbers and the smaller ones want to use the Metro Survey Area numbers. And of course, very small stations don't want to use numbers at all! The point is, you know where your customers are coming from, so you can decide which is best for you. Again, just make sure you are comparing apples to apples so you're not left gnawing on cores.

A Little Static Goes a Long Way

Now that you've gotten the best possible deal and placed your spots so that you'll get some impact, it's a good idea to listen to those spots when they're aired. You'll find that there will be some technical problems with the spots. One day the DJ may clip a few seconds off the beginning or ending of your spot. Or it may get caught in the machine and part of it may sound garbled like talking under water. Regardless of the mistake, complain about it to your sales rep. In most cases you'll get a freebie called a "make-good."

When you write or produce a commercial, you want to do everything in your power to get your spot noticed. Remember, there's a lot of competition out there for a piece of the listener's brain. The game is "Hey, look at me!" One good way to get a little extra attention is to produce a 25-second spot that allows for a 5-second live announcement or "tag" at the end.

There are a number of reasons for this. When commercials are played, they are done during a commercial break consisting of maybe four to six spots at one time. People have a tendency to remember the first and the last spot more than the ones in the middle.

By having a live tag, you are more likely to be placed at the end of all the commercials. That's because the DJ plays your commercial on a tape cartridge or *cart,* which looks very similar to an eight-track tape. These carts are placed in a machine and all the DJ has to do is punch a button and it starts instantly. Now, while DJs are doing this, they're also cuing up the next record, writing in the log, answering the request line, and trying to line up a date for Saturday night. They generally won't break into the middle of a series of commercials to do a live tag, but will wait until the end when they have to announce the time and weather before the next song. It's just a lot easier for them that way, and that's fine with us. Not only is your placement better during the break, but the "live" announcement adds a little more spontaneity and excitement.

Now if you're really slick, provide the station with a radio script or copy that has the live tag written for them. On your copy, misspell a few words to make it hard for the DJ to read. Write the tag so that it's difficult to pronounce. Use tongue twisters or sexual innuendo. When the jocks mess up a spot, they often take two or three passes at the tag and then joke about it for some time after to make the best of their "boo-boo." This draws much attention to your spot and impacts the listener. It's that fine line between the commercial and the entertainment. Remember, they tune out the commercials but they tune in to listen to music, the news, and the jocks. So, they just happen to joke about your spot. Wonderful!

When you hear the jock mess up the spot, you'll naturally be thrilled to death. But you want your sales rep to think you're very upset. Ask for a make-good!

A nightclub was working with a very limited budget. They produced their own 30-second spot, but not with a live tag. They provided the finished tape to the station. It turned out somehow that the tape contained three seconds of static at the end, obliterating part of the address. We don't really know if it was a mistake or a trick they learned from Richard Nixon's secretary, but after 17 of the scheduled 20 spots were run, the owner called up the station and complained. Seventeen make-goods with no questions asked.

How to Create Impact with Radio Promotions

Promotions are what it's all about when it comes to radio advertising. When done correctly, absolutely nothing can surpass the effectiveness of a radio promotion. It's also the one area that most of the mass media haven't the flexibility to provide.

The most common and most easily acquired promotion is the live remote broadcast from your location—a great traffic builder. For three hours or so, the DJ actually makes a number of live broadcasts from your store. That's nice. But probably the real reason behind the success of radio remote is that it's one of the few times a station will place a number of your commercials in a short period of time. Usually, you start promoting the remote a week before, and the spots run heavily all week long. You've made such an impact that many people may stop out. The jock being present and doing the live broadcast is the icing on the cake.

Usually, when you buy a remote package, you not only get a number of spots, but the station will also provide a number of short, live announcements called "promos" or "liners" that say that their jock will be there. It's to the station's advantage to have a good turnout because they don't want to look bad, either. Not only does it raise revenue for the station, but the DJ makes some extra bucks and the station gets extra exposure.

Stations are getting more and more sophisticated in conducting their remote broadcasts. Most used to do it over a regular telephone that was patched through the studio. Now they have elaborate remote trucks or vans with microwave transmitting capabilities so that the remote has the same sound of high quality as does the studio. Most people think this is a plus. Not so. What's the game we are playing? "Hey, look at me!" Or in this case, "Listen to me!" That tinny sound of a DJ on a phone tells the listener that this must be a special event because he sounds so different. So, insist on a telephone and not a remote truck. You might even ask them to give you a little break in the price since it's not as much trouble for them. It doesn't hurt to ask.

The next thing about a remote is that the jock will want to call from a phone in the back room where it's nice and quiet. Wrongo! Place him right out in the crowd. Get that background noise on the air. The jock will have to speak louder to be heard over the noise. All the better. Adds excitement. If you're going to have a party, sound like it.

Lastly, when the DJ arrives at your store, take the time to show him or her around. Explain what merchandise you want pushed during the broadcast. If it's a car, for example, have the jock drive it around for a minute on the parking lot to get the feel of it. Stereo equipment? Let the jock hear the quality. When the jock is talking on the air the jock often mentions having personally driven it, or listened to it, or whatever. A great way to get a testimonial from a recognized personality. Moral: Turn the jock on before he or she turns the mike on.

If It Works

The concept of the remote should be a big party. Giveaways, free soft drinks and balloons, ridiculously priced loss leaders and so on. If you do everything right and you sell a lot of merchandise, the first person who will want to know is the sales rep who sold you the remote. Never say you're thrilled beyond belief. Even if there are hundreds of people running around, act low key. Say you have to wait until the final figures are in before you'll pass judgment. Then say later that it was okay, or marginal. Nothing to get excited about, but you might want to try it again.

If you show excitement, jump up and down, and kiss your sales rep on both cheeks because you're making so much money. The rep will get excited, too. And, two things might happen. That rep will want to raise the ante the next time because it worked so well—and will go to all your competitors telling them how successful it was and why they should do it too.

If It Doesn't Work

Now let's suppose that it fell flat on its assets. Was the problem unavoidable, like a blizzard or hurricane? If not, then it's safe to assume that the station doesn't pull all that well with their remotes. You learned a little more about the station, but that may not be all that comforting knowing how much money you doled out to conduct this fiasco.

What do you do? Revenge? In a fashion, but not with the station. Sure, they're the enemy, but this problem presents a unique opportunity.

Write a letter to the sales manager telling them what a fantastic job they did for you. Be sure to mention that you made a ton of sales as a result of using a remote on their station. Really ham it up. What happens? They're off selling the same promotion to all of your competitors! Why not let them waste their money for awhile?

That brings to mind a related streetfighting technique done by an attorney. He wrote a real nice letter to a station with a very aggressive sales force. The letter complimented them on some programs they had run. The letter was written on the attorney's stationery. We know for a fact that this particular attorney hated the station management with a passion because he had worked for them years before and had left on not-too-good terms. Why did he write the letter? One reason might be because the sales manager had copies of the letter made for each of her salespeople. On their regular calls, they of course showed all their clients and potential clients the nice letter. That attorney received free exposure to every business in that community. Could he have asked for a better target audience? A better price?

Playing to Radio Station Self-Interest

Next to selling air time, radio stations love to play for themselves. They are forever looking for ways they can create excitement about their station. If you can help them do it, there is a good opportunity for you to get free exposure.

The free exposure, however, comes from an entirely different department of the station. Up until now we have been dealing with the sales department. But a different department isn't worried so much about commissions, quotas, or make-goods. Now you are dealing with the programming department, which is responsible for the station's giveaways, contests, parties, and even the music they play. The programming department has a certain amount of available air time for this purpose. And if you can tie in with these promotion spots, you not only get the free exposure, but you get greater impact. These commercials aren't perceived as commercials. Listeners tune out commercials, but they listen very carefully when the station is running a contest to give away a car, or throwing a party with drinks compliments of the station. It's part of the entertainment just like the music, news, and weather. Even during the dreaded commercial-free music sweeps, the "promos" are still aired, thus reinforcing to their listeners that commercials about the station aren't really commercials.

Not all types of businesses can be in a position to help a radio station promote itself. But anything related to the food-service or entertainment industries automatically qualifies. That's not to say that it's impossible for an auto parts store or laundromat. But let's give you a story about one nightclub that turned itself around with this concept. Then you take it from there.

The jocks love the arrangement primarily because they will be renumerated for their personal appearances. For three hours at $75 an hour, the DJ came to this nightclub and played the records. This may sound a bit overpriced, but you have to consider that the station wants a good turnout so they'll look good. So they played a ten-second live announcement promoting the fact that their DJ was going to be at the nightclub on this night. They placed this promo once an hour, 24 hours a day, for five days. In this particular market, an equivalent to about $2,000 of advertising a week, if you had to buy it.

Unfortunately, to get this deal, you can't get by the sales department totally unscathed. They know what you are getting for nothing and they want their share. So throw them a bone. In this case, the budget wasn't set up front. We would have been perfectly happy with just the promotional announcement and without the paid-for spots. It wasn't to be. In this situation, we negotiated the smallest amount first, then dealt with how many spots we got for it later.

You have to be careful not to give your sales reps the feeling that they're unnecessary parasites. It's just not true. Often, it's your sales rep who sets up the meeting for you to get to meet with the programming director. Again, get close to the enemy and you'll learn much about their allies, too.

Once you've arranged for a meeting, the program directors have to be handled differently from sales reps. Their motivations are entirely different. While a sales rep is motivated by greed in the form of a commission, the programming director is motivated by ego. He or she is on the radio for the glory. If they were interested in making a lot of money, they'd have joined the sales staff. They like it when people call them up. They like to see their faces on large billboards. They're the closest thing to a celebrity in your city, and they love it.

How did we find all this out? The hard way! We wanted to put on a big promotion for this same nightclub. An early New Year's Eve party in October. We knew it would be something their customers would eat up. By this time we were dealing with the program director directly and called him to tell him about our fantastic idea. He said he would think about it. He sounded unimpressed. This was the premiere idea of the century and he wanted to think about it? We hung up the phone and knew immediately what we had done wrong. It wasn't *his* idea! We hadn't played to his ego.

Once we realized that the premier promotion of the century had been blown by the premier blunder of the decade, we sprang into action in true streetfighting form. At once, we were on the phone to our sales rep. We told him that we would like to arrange a meeting between us, the client, the promotion director, and himself. We also let him know that we wanted to have another promotion for the nightclub and that our budget for this promotion was more than last time. That got his attention and cooperation. The meeting was set. We rehearsed. The client rehearsed. The sales rep's calculator was set on overload in anticipation of a big sale, and the programming director was led to our table at the restaurant where just six months before we had discussed a variety of other promotions that we contemplated doing throughout the year.

The meeting began with the usual small talk as we ordered lunch. We always order big at these meetings. It's not that they make us unusually hungry, but the station always meets us where they have a trade agreement with the restaurant. Halfway through the chicken Kiev, we told the program director that we really wanted to have the early New Year's Eve party just as he suggested.

"I suggested?"

"Sure, don't you remember? We had a meeting about six months ago right here in this same restaurant and you suggested having an early New Year's Eve party and we thought it was crazy. Well, we don't think it's so crazy now."

Then the client jumped in and reinforced it. The sales rep even reminded him about the meeting, and he wasn't even at the rehearsal.

We finally convinced him that the early New Year's Eve party was his idea. It turned out to be one of the most successful promotions ever conducted at this club.

This same principle was used for a travel agency that had overbooked on a singles cruise to the Bahamas. After their advertising efforts had failed and they were left with 30 cabins still to sell, they approached us to help them save their sinking ship.

In our initial interview with them, we found out that travel agencies are given freebies for these types of package deals. The more people they book, the more free cruises they get.

After uncovering that valuable piece of information, we talked with the program director of a rock station. He just happened to be single. We suggested that his listeners would really like an opportunity to win a free cruise to the Bahamas valued at over $1,500. In addition, his listeners would go absolutely nuts when they found out that he would be on the cruise as well. His eyes opened wide. He loved the idea and made it an official station promotion. Using 30-second promos and 10-second live liners, we were able to create enough awareness to save the travel agent's rudder on this venture. The cost was zero.

Not all station promotions are a good medium for all merchants. If the station approaches you first, you can bet your bottom line that the sales department is behind it, and it's going to cost you some big bucks. But, there are exceptions—station promotions and special packages designed specifically for the benefit of the station and not necessarily for the client.

Even if your business doesn't lend itself to an all-out promotion by the station, as a nightclub or travel agency does, you can still take advantage of the programming department. Jocks love to give merchandise away on the air. It helps them build their audience. When providing the station with giveaway merchandise, you not only want them to mention you every time they promote the event, but you also should try to get them to give an equal value in air time as well.

Then, instead of giving the merchandise directly to the station, give them certificates or letters so that the lucky winners have to come in to your store to pick it up. At least a few more people will have walked into your store, and who knows—they might buy something while they're there.

Trading and Bartering

We mentioned quite a bit about trading your products and services for advertising time. It's a great way to get the advertising you need at a lower cost. At the same time, you might be able to unload some merchandise that's been on your books for awhile. Instead of selling it at cost or below just to unload it, you might actually get full retail for it in the form of radio advertising. It's much better on the cash flow when you can pay the media bills right out of accounts payable. But as many advantages as there are to trading, you must be careful. There are many ways the station can rip you off.

First of all, consider the type of merchandise you're trading. Many times the station will come to you for a specific item that they need. If that item is not one of particularly high profit margin, you might be able to negotiate more than the retail value for it. If they want it badly enough, they'll pay for it (in air time). A radio station wished to trade with a tailor for a custom suit. Most of the cost for that particular item is labor—his. That particular station wasn't the best target audience for his product, but the station was persistent. He finally was offered a trade ten times the retail of his custom suit! At that price, almost any radio station can be efficient.

Figure your actual cost in this advertising. Just like the tailor, this particular station may not be the best for your target audience. But once you figure out your cost per thousand at the traded rate, it might be a very good buy. Restaurants are the first types of businesses radio stations offer trades with. They take their clients there for lunch to entice them to buy. Set the rules up front with the station. (Like tipping your waitresses 20 percent cash.)

Health clubs and dance or aerobic classes are high-profit items as it were, because you have little or no direct cost against each purchase. You just place one more person in the class, so the air time is practically free in that situation.

On the other end of the spectrum, many appliances are low-profit items. It may not be worth it to you in that situation to trade merchandise for a marginal station, unless you arrange something like the tailor did to make it worth his while.

Second-Class Citizen

Once the station finally gets the trade, they have a tendency to treat you like a second-class citizen. We have found agreements used by stations for trading that flat out ripped the merchants off. The station received quality merchandise or service just like a cash customer, but did not reciprocate. First of all, you can be preempted by any cash advertiser. That means you get only the leftovers. Or they may only give you the spot at the single highest rate on the card, and also charge for production. When they tried to pull this stunt with a family restaurant client, we told them that we would trade with them; but they can only be seated after everyone else and only eat what everyone left at their plates. They got our message.

The time to negotiate the terms of the trade is when you set it up. Once they have the trade, they know they can give you whatever rate per spot they choose. So, negotiate your spot cost as part of the deal. If you're buying time at the station and getting "the brother-in-law rates," make them aware that you expect the same rates for your traded time as well.

Teamwork

By teaming up with other advertisers, many times you can increase your frequency and awareness without increasing your advertising budget. At the same time we were consulting our nightclub client, we were asked by a promoter of an exhibition NBA basketball game for some help.

By working with both clients, we were able to increase their visibility tremendously at no additional cost. The nightclub was getting all those free live announcements we mentioned earlier. We told the jock who was going to be out at the club that he would be able to give away tickets to the game to his fans at the club. Naturally, he wanted to promote the fact that he was going to give away these tickets. He felt that it would bring more people to the club to see him. So for one week, the sporting event was mentioned 70 times on that station. It wasn't a commercial for the event, but by mentioning that they were giving away tickets to this game, a great deal of awareness was created.

In return, the promoter mentioned at the end of all their commercials that there would be an after-game party at this nightclub. It was the classic everyone-wins situation. The club received free mentions in the sporting event's advertising and the sporting event received free mentions in the club's advertising. An interesting by-product of that cooperative venture was that the nightclub was packed right after the game. Not only was this promotion head and shoulders above the rest, but so were some of the players who showed up at the club.

Mentioning each other in advertising is really a great way to increase your exposure at no additional cost. Another technique can be used to double the frequency of your spot schedule. We first discovered it when we were consulting a small strip center. Promotions and events were worthless for this little shopping center. We bought 60-second spots and gave each merchant 19 seconds to sell whatever they wished. The last three seconds were used to announce the name of the center as the sponsor for the commercials.

This arrangement intrigued us. There was a big advantage to these merchants. The cost of a 30-second spot in radio is just a little less than the cost of the 60-second spot. If the cost of 30 is $20, the 60may be only $5 more. So what would happen if two merchants, each having a 30-second spot, would splice their commercials together to form one 60-second spot and split the cost of the schedule? Well, first of all, the station would reject it. It's called *piggybacking*, and naturally the station frowns on this practice because they feel it is money out of their pockets—and it is! To get around this problem, you simply make an association of yourself.

Making an Association of Yourself

The reason the station accepted the strip center's ads was because they had a legitimate reason for advertising in a group. And they had a merchants' association from which all the media bills were paid. So if you were to get a small group of merchants together who are not competitive, but who still have the same basic target audience, you might be able to find a loophole.

During a given month, each member of the group agreed to spend $500 on this particular radio station. If you're sharing a spot with another merchant, you have 28 seconds to sell what you will. Your partner has the same, and the remaining time is used to identify the association. That's required by the station to make this thing work. So if you were to place your $500 by yourself, you might get a total of 25 commercials at your $20 per-spot cost. But, when you combine your effort with another member of your newly formed association, the situation changes. Now you buy 60-second spots instead of 30s. You're paying $25 per spot, but now the total expenditure with the station is $1,000 instead of $500. Now you get 40 commercials instead of 25 and you still pay only $500 each.

Many times you can say what you have to in less than 30 seconds. Twenty-second spots are not available on most radio stations. But if you have two other members in your group with equally brief messages, you can work together to air three different 19-second messages in the same 60-second spot. Now you have a total of $1,500 to spend among the three of you—and that's 60 spots.

There's yet another advantage to this group buying program. Stations lower their cost per spot when you increase the number of spots you buy in a given seven-day period. The 6-time rate, which is what you call it when you buy six spots in a week, will have a little higher cost per spot than the 12-time rate. You often get the price breaks at the 18- and 24-time rate, too. By working together with other merchants, you'll stand a better chance of getting the better prices because you'll be able to afford more spots in a week. That could add as much as 10 percent to your schedule.

As we said before, the station doesn't take kindly to this type of activity. So you need to form a legitimate merchants' association. Meet once a month. Elect officers, and do whatever it takes to make it legitimate. You might even have an attorney draw up the charter for you. Then, to really make it stick, have the association hire a small advertising agency to place the time for you. That will usually get past the station because the agency will accept the responsibility for the group.

As for the name of your association, you could always choose the name of your street, like "The Main Street Merchants' Association." You could even choose the section of town you're located in, like "The Northeast Merchants' Association." The association should be made up of merchants who are not competitors, but are complimentary to each other. For example, look at a major department store. You can't compete with their advertising budget by yourself, but if you break it down, what do you have? An appliance store, hardware store, clothing store, lawn and garden store, and so on. For every department they have, you can find a merchant that wants a piece of the action. By working together with a dozen or so other merchants, you have as much, if not more, to offer as one department store does. It's certainly a cross-promotion on a different level, but now is the time you need each other to survive. Oh, by the way, one last trick. When you set up this association and decide you really don't need that advertising agency, you might be able to form an in-house agency and collect the 15 percent commission for the association—but that's another story.

8

TELEVISION

Without a doubt, the most powerful advertising medium known is television. The sum total of all the other forms of advertising—sight, sound, motion, and color—are all delivered into the living rooms of almost every living soul in the country.

Television has the ability to demonstrate your product to a large number of people. It has a higher degree of credibility than most other forms of mass advertising available in your community—an advertiser's dream.

But the dream is rapidly turning into a nightmare. Visions of skyrocketing costs and a declining audience are making this awesome medium lose much of its impact. But through these changes, though potentially devastating to the large mass retailers who have relied on its power for so long, the smaller merchants will see much greater opportunity. As TV begins to self-destruct, there will be a great equalizing factor that will force these retailing giants to search for alternative ways to reach their customers, ways you'll already be implementing as a streetfighter. And when the committee has to meet to approve each and every little promotion, from a simple coupon exchange to an elaborate community involvement program, you'll have the upper hand. You can act at a moment's notice.

It's Wired

Why is TV going down the tubes? The audiences are being divided into many different special-interest groups, which is referred to as "fractionalization." The primary source of this problem is due to the increased penetration of cable TV. Where you once had the choice in your city of watching three network affiliate stations, possibly an independent and maybe a PBS station, you now have 20 or 30 stations from which to choose. In the not-too-distant future, you may have well over 100 stations to choose from.

With so many choices, people will find shows that suit their particular interest instead of just what the networks are sending down, such as old "McHale's Navy" reruns on the local independent.

New cable networks are springing up and chipping away at the neworks. Names like CNN, ESPN, HBO, Cinemax, Showtime, USA, WTBS, The Movie Channel, The English Channel, and the list goes on.

Aside from cable, the attack continues from the air, via satellite-transmitted programs and networks like ON-TV. It looks like the satellites are going to cause as much trouble for the cable companies as the cable people have caused for the local affiliates.

Then there are other distractions—home video games, computers, video discs, and video tape players. All of these make your TV commercials that much less effective. Every time your TV set has another use, it affects the impact of local TV commercials. Zenith has a TV out that runs the telephone through it. So if your commercial happens to be on just as somebody is getting a phone call, guess who wins the attention of that viewer—a viewer you paid a lot of money to reach.

And the problem doesn't end there. There's another aspect of TV that's a little frightening. (That's if you spend any money on TV advertising at all.) It was called "zapping" in an article that appeared in *TV Guide,* and it relates directly to remote control. More and more sets are being sold with remote control devices, and a favorite pastime of many viewers is to watch more than one show at a time. This usually occurs during the commercials. So not only do you have to contend with people getting up during the commercials to get a beer, or relieve themselves from the last one they had, but you also have to deal with their changing the station to catch a few minutes of another show.

Still Has the Power

We're not suggesting that TV advertising is not worth using on a local basis, we just want you to be aware of how rapidly it's changing.

When your sales rep tells you there's good news—the rates were held to same as last year, don't get too excited. With the viewer attrition rate the way it is, you'll still be paying more for less.

But you can still get some good action from TV if you use it right. How long it will last is anybody's guess. So this chapter will be devoted to showing you a few techniques for getting more out of your TV budget. However, each market is different and you have to keep up on what's happening in your market. What's your cable penetration? That is, what percentage of all the homes in your viewing area is hooked up to cable? In some cities it could be as high as 75 percent, in others, as low as 3 percent. Keep an eye on and try to track the results you're getting from your TV advertising. When the return on investment gets out of hand, be prepared for some kind of alternative game plan.

Buying Time

The basic negotiation strategies for TV are the same as for radio. You'll find that you get better response from your sales rep if you set your budget up front, then start negotiating more spots or better positions. TV, like radio, is a perishable commodity. The price fluctuates with supply and demand. When a station has a great deal of time sold, they probably won't give you the time of day. But when the logs look a little on the bare side, they'll come crawling to your store with their tongues dragging and an outstretched arm. It's very possible that Dr. Jekyll was a TV sales rep at one time—or was it Mr. Hyde?

The objective of buying TV time is to reach as many people in your target audience as possible for the least amount of money. You want to reach them as many times as possible for what the budget will allow. So let's say you're going to spend $1,000 on TV to advertise a sale. Three stations make proposals for $1,000. How do you figure which station is giving you the most for your money? Just as we figured in radio, the cost per thousand or CPM is a way to compare.

The CPM lets you know how much it's going to cost for you to reach each group of 1,000 people. Just because one station's shows are rated best in your market doesn't mean that they're the best buy for you. Remember, you're dealing with limited funds. Don't worry about rating points, target rating points, shares, or any other numbers a TV rep may throw at you. The important figure for you is the cost per thousand for your target audience. It's figured in the same way as it is for radio, and it's really not necessary for you to know how to do it yourself. Most TV stations now have computers that can do that for you. Just make sure that all stations are using the same rating book for the same month and year.

The TV stations generally subscribe to two ratings services—Arbitron and Nielsen. Which one is best is anybody's guess. If one station shows better ratings in one book than another, that's the one they'll usually try to use. Since you're using this only as a guideline, pick a current survey and survey company and stick with it for all the stations that give you a proposal.

Figures 8-1 and 8-2 show some excerpts from Arbitron. Look at them briefly, then forget them. Most of the numbers don't mean anything to you. They may not mean much to the people at the stations unless you're located in a top 50 market!

Once you tell your sales rep your target audience, they'll usually try to give you shows that do well for that group. Aside from the cost per thousand, you also have to concern yourself with the actual cost per spot. For big budgets it's not necessary, but for your $1,000, it is. If a certain program has a very low CPM but costs $400 for one 30-second spot, you wouldn't get enough frequency to drive home the message enough to get any action from it.

Just as in radio, you need frequency to make your TV schedule work. If you have only 1,000 bucks to spend, you might have to deal with spots that cost $50 to $60 or less, then cram them all into a four- or five-day period to make an impact.

To get the best deal on a small budget, place all your money on one station. You'll usually get a better deal by providing $1,000 to one station than you would if you split it three ways. All or nothing makes your rep work harder for the buy.

Run of Station

Stations offer a program called ROS, or run of station. This is where your spots cost a certain price each and can fall anytime within a prespecified time perimeter. If you buy an ROS from 4:00 P.M. to 12:00 midnight, for example, the cost per spot will be more than if the time perimeter was from sign-on to sign-off. By "bracketing" the time

Weekly Program Estimates — Program Audience Estimates

TIME AND STATION		TELE-CASTS		WEEK-BY-WEEK ADI TV HH RATINGS				ADI TV HH			METRO TV HH			TV HH	PERSONS						WOMEN							WKG WMN 18+
DAY	PROGRAM	# OF WKS	# OF QTR-HRS	WK1 11/3	WK2 11/10	WK3 11/17	WK4 11/24	RTG	SHR	HUT	RTG	SHR	HUT		TOT 2+	18+	18-49	12-24	12-34	1-34	TOT 18+	18-49	12-24	12-34	18-34	25-49	25-54	18+
	(col #) 1	2	3	4				5	6	7	8	9	10	11	12	13	14	15	16	17	18	19	20	21	22	23		24
RELATIVE STD-ERR 25%	THRESHOLDS 50% (1σ)													11 / 2	26 / 6	17 / 4	14 / 3	18 / 4	16 / 4	15 / 3	13 / 3	12 / 3	17 / 4	16 / 4	15 / 3		23	12 / 3
8:00P WGR / WLVB																												
SAT	DFRNT STROKS	2	4					20	35	58	21	36	60	130	248	161	68	44	67	31	95	45	18	40	19	40	49	13
SUN	CHIPS	2	12					16	23	68	17	25	70	100	213	153	92	61	89	58	80	46	31	33	25	33	38	17
SUN	NBC SUN MOV	2	16					12	19	67	15	22	68	80	145	121	82	35	70	55	61	42	11	34	30	34	41	22
AVG	PRES REAGAN	2	4					13	21	61	13	21	59	80	155	128	65	19	39	29	75	34	10	29	18	29	34	17
MON	^CBS NW SP RP	4	4					12	26	44	15	23	63	75	102	84	46	20	41	30	47	33	17	21	21	23	23	14
	SQUARE PEGS	4	8					14	22	64	16	25	63	91	172	128	93	49	88	70	74	52	32	41	25	30	35	19
TUE	BRNG BCK ALV	3	12					17	26	61	11	18	60	68	121	90	59	25	50	38	48	32	12	21	21	24	27	10
	^SPC MV PRSNT	4	12					17	26	65	17	28	63	108	203	183	90	34	78		106	56	23	47	30	47	47	18
WED	^BLUE-GRAY	3	12					13	20	71	12	19	64	184	361	297	151	78	126		151	56		78		86	86	
	7BRDES 7BROS	3	12					13	20	63	12	18	64	82	167	128	59	35	66	51	73	45	23		30	36	36	18
THU	^7BRDES 7BROS	3	12					13	17	66	12	17	62	109	207	157	80	56	65		80	32	22	35		30	33	
	MAGNUM PI	3	12					28	37	80	25	40	62	158	289	244	123	55	102		135	66	18		35	54	66	28
	^SPC MV PRSNT	3	12					15	24	57	13	24	55	101	229	172	83	38	67		110	52	21	27	42	42	53	24
FRI	DUKES HAZARD	4	20					18	28	56	17	28	53	96	206	110	68	43	67	65	54	32	27		44	26	30	12
SAT	WALT DISNEY	3	16					26	41	65	25	39	66	87	194	139	72	22	48	78	78	44	12		65	27	31	22
SUN	ARCHIES PLCE	3	12					16	27	60	14	24	66	117	197	171	72	61	111	40	101	43			40	33	43	17
AVG	^BLUE-GRAY	1	12					12	28	45	12	26	45	169	307	279	143	62	111	79	167	88	36	40	79	59	73	26
AVG	CBS NW SP RP	2	32					25	39	67	26	39	66	169	311	270	141	28	111	27	148	79	14	21	88	21	23	13
AVG	SPC MV PRSNT	3	32					26	41	65	16	60	45	77	219	176	90	36	78	65	109	54	18	37	54	41	51	24
WKBW																												
MON	^PRES REAGAN	1	2					14	23	61	16	26	60	95	138	110	40	20	28	39	60	21	8	19		31	31	16
	THT INCRDBLE	4	14					18	26	65	15	24	64	92	173	136	69	25	52	77	77	36	34		45	36	43	
TUE	CNISUS BSKBL	1	8					20	32	65	22	33	67	115	221	159	114	59	100	85	85	65	18		29	54	51	
WED	HAPPY DAYS	3	12					17	30	62	16	25	60	132	263	173	88	66	72	99	99	48	24	24		38	43	25
	GOLD MONKEY	3	12					18	32	66	13	21	59	66	184	141	59	39	63	76	76	28	18		29	22	31	23
THU	JOANI-CHACHI	4	8					17	30	61	18	32	56	79	146	104	47	20	33	60	60	49	24		24		39	15
	^PRES REAGAN	2	2					17	30	56	13	21	61	111	218	175	80	34	61	104	104	38		30	48	36	48	16
FRI	BENSON	4	16					16	25	68	18	32	56	106	203	173	73	42	97	92	92	59	21	23		26	32	18
SAT	T J HOOKER	4	16					16	27	61	16	26	70	112	244	183	111	59		96	96	67	20	36		45	21	29
SUN	MATT HOUSTON	3	12					17	28	59	17	30	63	81	142	118	43	12	20	68	68	25	23	14	15	23	35	7
AVG	PRES REAGAN																											
WUTV																												
MON	^8 OCLOCK MOV	4	38					4	4	66	3	5	66	18	31	28	14	8	11	8	11	5	3	2	3	4	5	3
TUE	^8 OCLOCK MOV	4	36					6	8	64	6	9	64	30	48	44	27	10	24	19	19	14	4	9	4	10	12	5
WED	^8 OCLOCK MOV	4	34					5	7	62	6	9	65	31	57	47	47	11	18	18	24	16	8	11	8	10	12	4
THU	^8 OCLOCK MOV	4	39					5	8	58	4	7	62	33	51	44	24	9	20	15	21	11	5	7	5	8	10	4
FRI	^8 OCLOCK MOV‡	4	30					6	5	59			58	26	41	33	20	12	18	13	18	11	6	7	6	5	6	4
SAT	SILNT CRISIS‡	3	4					1	1	57	1	1	61	6	6	6	2	1	1	1	2	1						
SUN	700 CLUB SA	4	18					1	1	69	1	1	70	3	6	3	2		1	1	4	1					1	
SUN	700 CLUB SU		24																									
AVG	8 OCLOCK MOV‡	4	177					4	6	63	5	7	63	26	45	39	22	10	18	15	18	11	5	7		8	9	4

Figure 8-1

© Arbitron Ratings Company, 1982. Used with permission for educational purposes only.

177

Average Quarter-Hour and Cume Listening Estimates

MONDAY-FRIDAY
6.00AM-10.00AM

STATION CALL LETTERS	MEN 25-49 TOTAL AREA		MEN 25-49 METRO SURVEY AREA				MEN 25-54 TOTAL AREA		MEN 25-54 METRO SURVEY AREA				MEN 35-64 TOTAL AREA		MEN 35-64 METRO SURVEY AREA			
	AVG. PERS (00)	CUME PERS (00)	AVG. PERS (00)	CUME PERS (00)	AVG. PERS RTG.	AVG. PERS SHR.	AVG. PERS (00)	CUME PERS (00)	AVG. PERS (00)	CUME PERS (00)	AVG. PERS RTG.	AVG. PERS SHR.	AVG. PERS (00)	CUME PERS (00)	AVG. PERS (00)	CUME PERS (00)	AVG. PERS RTG.	AVG. PERS SHR.
WBBF	21	176	21	176	1.3	5.3	28	202	28	202	1.5	6.0	29	151	29	151	1.9	8.1
WCMF	40	253	38	244	2.3	9.6	40	253	38	244	2.0	8.2	7	64	7	64	.5	1.9
WDKX	10	48	10	48	.6	2.5	10	48	10	48	.5	2.2	9	28	9	28	.6	2.5
WECQ	1	18	1	18	.1	.3	1	18	1	18	.1	.2	3	17	3	17	.2	.8
WEZO	27	199	27	199	1.6	6.8	45	300	44	295	2.3	9.5	58	379	57	374	3.8	15.9
WFLC	11	38	11	38	.7	2.8	11	38	11	38	.6	2.4	18	66	14	59	.9	3.9
WHAM	64	397	45	293	2.7	11.4	74	464	55	355	2.9	11.8	84	446	61	359	4.1	17.0
WHFM	17	145	17	135	1.0	4.3	17	151	17	141	.9	3.7	6	43	6	43	.4	1.7
WMJQ	24	210	24	200	1.5	6.1	24	210	24	200	1.3	5.2	3	53	3	53	.2	.8
WNYR	34	185	30	172	1.8	7.6	36	209	32	196	1.7	6.9	38	200	24	170	1.6	6.7
WPXN	10	68	10	68	.6	2.5	18	100	18	100	1.0	3.9	25	139	25	139	1.7	7.0
WPXY	24	197	24	197	1.5	6.1	29	221	29	221	1.5	6.2	13	111	13	111	.9	3.6
WRTK	1	17	1	17	.1	.3	2	30	2	30	.1	.4	2	36	2	36	.1	.6
WVOR	77	399	74	362	4.5	18.7	87	441	84	404	4.5	18.1	37	217	37	217	2.5	10.3
WWWG	1	28	1	28	.1	.3	1	28	1	28	.1	.2		6		6		
WYLF	4	41	3	32	.2	.8	7	66	5	51	.3	1.1	17	120	11	90	.7	3.1
WBEN	2	26					4	33					10	58	6	25	.4	1.7
WBEN FM	2	21	1	11	.1	.3	3	36	2	26	.1	.4	2	21	2	21	.1	.6
WKBW	7	82	2	24	.1	.5	8	94	2	29	.1	.4	10	85	1	20	.1	.3
WKFM	3	18					3	18					2	9				
WPCX	3	59	3	39	.2	.8	3	59	3	39	.2	.6	13	78	2	40	.1	.6

© *Arbitron Ratings Company, 1982. Used with permission for educational purposes only.*

Figure 8-2

period that your spots fall in, you can be somewhat assured that you'll get at least a few good spots. You might even get lucky and have some fall into news, prime, or prime access at the price of late-night spots. Much of it depends on the availabilities.

ROS can be a good deal for you if your spots don't fall after midnight each time. If you establish a good relationship with your sales reps, they can usually tell when you'll fare well on an ROS package.

The Most Powerful Person at the TV Station

Take a guess. Who do you think is the most powerful person at your local TV station, as far as an advertiser is concerned? The general manager? News director? Sales Manager? No! It's an underpaid, overworked, seldom-appreciated secretary who heads up the traffic department.

We found this out by accident a number of years ago when the station messed up an important schedule for a big client. It wasn't just a matter of running make-goods because the commercial was advertising a major promotion that was to begin on a specific date.

Naturally, the account executive wanted to salvage as much of the schedule as possible—not only to keep us from never using him again, but also because he made no commission if the spots didn't run. About half of the week-long schedule was missed and he invited us down to the station to see if we couldn't come up with some kind of solution.

Upon our arrival he ushered us into the traffic department, where the logs are written and stored on computer. We had no problem cramming as many spots into the remaining days as the log would allow. Since the spots were ROS, it was not only a matter of finding times, but of finding the best ones available.

Our person in traffic punched up the log on the computer screen. We started putting the spots into available areas, requesting all of the better times. We were even able to bump a competitor's ROS spot out of a prime-time position and reschedule it for a little after midnight.

By the time we were done scheduling the spots, our $2,500 schedule looked more like $25,000! We picked up a number of prime-time spots, early and late news, prime access, and early fringe. The original schedules called for spots to fall between 4:00 P.M. and sign-off. Normally, at least half the spots would fall in some of the not-so-great times. If the dollar amounts mean nothing to you, think of it as being able to reach ten times as many people.

So what started out as a complete disaster turned out to be one of the most effective time buys ever, not to mention an interesting learning experience.

The next day we sent the traffic secretary who had assisted us a nice bouquet of flowers thanking her for helping us out of a jam. She never forgot that. After that, we were on a first-name basis. When I bought an ROS schedule, I'd call down to the station and see what my chances were of getting decent positions. I never asked her to place the spots in any particular positions. But, by calling ahead, I let her know we had a schedule coming. We always seemed to get better-than-average positions for our clients.

If the log was tight and we couldn't get good positions, it was nice to know so we could get fixed positions, if necessary. Even though we had to pay a premium for those spots, we did it if we knew there was no way to get them otherwise.

Spreading the Word

We truly felt as if we had discovered a gold mine when we figured out how to get the most for our TV budget. But, we could do it only on one station. Would it work at the other stations? How do you create a near-disaster so you have the opportunity to establish a relationship with someone in traffic?

First, we went on a tour of the other station. Sales reps are always happy to show you around and let you look at all their fine technology. We made a point of making sure our tour included the traffic department. We were then introduced to all the people in the traffic department, and they explained how their department worked. We listened in awe as they went through the procedures on their computer terminals. We asked important questions like, "How are the spots scheduled in the log?" They told us that they were all done by computer, which automatically spreads the ROS spots equally so everyone gets their fair shot at the good times.

"What happens if a spot is missed? How do you get back in the log?" For that, they can do it manually if need be. We also found out that since the logs are done a few days ahead of time, we could find out where the spots are scheduled to fall by calling them up. They can then run a computer printout that will tell us exactly where they intend to place us. But with ROS spots, they're immediately preemptable if someone pays a fixed-position rate.

This started to paint a picture for us. We thanked them for their time and then were led to the conference room to view some garbage propaganda tape about how great their station was—but the donuts were free.

On the first occasion of placing an ROS schedule at that station, we made a phone call to the traffic department. We told the person there that we had a real problem, a life and death situation. We needed to find out the times the spots were running on this particular account because our client's wife wanted to see them. We stressed how important this was to us, almost near panic.

She ran the computer printout of the tentative schedule, which she read to us over the phone. Seemingly relieved after getting this information, we proceeded to thank her profusely for her help. After all, she probably saved the account for us, so she thought.

The next day—flowers. She called us up to thank us, which we insisted was not necessary, it should be us thanking her. From that point on we had a very wonderful working relationship. Of course, the client never even knew or cared about the printout. The only thing they cared about was seeing a nice return on their investment.

It never hurts to know people in important places—but you have to determine what is an important place.

10s, 30s, and 60s

In television, unlike radio, the cost of a 60-second commercial is normally twice that of a 30-second commercial. With the cost of TV, it's usually advisable to keep your message to 30 seconds, if possible, because you'll be able to afford twice as many commercials. Twice the frequency will increase your impact.

In TV you can buy 10-second spots, though there are generally not as many available. The cost is often half that of the 30-second rate at that time slot. Ten seconds is not a great deal of time to tell a message, but if you have a 10-second message, you would be wise to get twice the frequency over 30s, provided there is adequate availability.

10-Second Strategies

There are a couple of ways you can use 10-second spots very effectively. One is a "reminder" spot. First, a little math: Let's say you're going to buy twenty 30-second spots at a cost of $50 each. Total budget for the flight (all twenty spots) is $1,000. But if you take five of those spots and divide them into ten 10s without increasing your cost, you now have 25 commercials for the same $1,000.

Your 10-second spots should be reminder spots, giving only the vital information that was in the 30s. For the best impact, place the 10s so that they fall an hour or less after the 30, preferably during the same show. In that case, you make almost the same impact as two 30-second commercials, but at a savings of $25.

Even if the spots are reversed, and the 10 plays before the 30, the 10 will have a tendency to help that 30 make a greater impact. We can't repeat enough that on a limited budget, frequency is vital to effectiveness. If a person sees your spot just once or twice, it is not enough to cause action. The audience must be bombarded as much as possible to get the most out of your budget. The 10s used properly can help you stretch your budget.

Simple Messages

You may have a very simple message that requires only a 10-second spot. That happened to a lawn and garden client. They carried Toro lawnmowers, as did most of their competitors. Toro supplied each of its dealers with a video tape of a professionally produced Toro spot that allowed for the dealer tag during the last five seconds. Toro provided a very attractive co-op package that allowed their dealers to get reimbursed a large percentage of their advertising used for Toro.

In addition, Toro was buying many spots regionally, and they rotated the names of their area dealers at the end. Plus, they were running a heavy network schedule as well. There was no doubt that the name Toro was getting a great deal of awareness.

This garden shop figured that since all their competitors were playing the Toro spot, which was designed primarily to sell the benefits of owning a Toro, and the regional and national Toro advertising was doing the same, there was no need for them to run the same 30-second spots. The awareness and demand for the product was already being created. They came in with 10-second spots and outdoor billboards that simply stated that they were the number one Toro dealer in the area! So while everyone else was helping to create a demand for the product, they were just telling the consumer the best place to buy it!

When you have a simple message, no use wasting expensive time if you don't have to.

Shared I.D.'s

Some stations have available a little gem called a "shared I.D." Once an hour, the stations are required by the FCC to identify themselves. They come on for four or five seconds and tell you what their call letters are. They also have a slide that appears on the screen, which shows you the call letters, as well.

To share that slide is pretty cheap, though it may be different from station to station. (When we've used it, the cost was 10 percent of the 30-second rate.) All you get is a slide of your logo next to the station's logo. But if you're looking for gross impressions, it's a good one.

Not only did one of our clients use this to build up general awareness for their name, but the slide they provided the station with was very interesting. The logo was shot on a white background, which came out clear when developed. So when the slide came on, the light from the TV set became very bright. Enough so that it could wake up the soundest snoozer just in time to catch a glimpse of the logo.

Planning Ahead

Since TV rates are seasonal, the time to negotiate is when they're most desperate. If possible, you'll find it to your advantage to plan your TV schedules six months to a year in advance. That way you can lock the stations in to the lower rates during the expensive times like Christmas.

Probably the best time of the year to negotiate is the beginning or middle of January. The station would just be coming off of record sales from November and December, and looking at a half-empty log into January.

Co-Op Advertising, Share the Wealth

In many businesses, especially those in considered purchases, the manufacturer provides co-op funds that reimburse you for part—and sometimes all—of your advertising expenses. An appliance store found itself in a unique situation that allowed them to make a profit before they sold the first piece of merchandise.

White-Westinghouse allowed a 75 percent co-op allotment for their dryers and ranges. That's quite a bit of savings. At the same time, the gas company had a co-op program that allowed between 25 and 33 percent reimbursement on advertising gas appliances. Through a careful negotiation between the two suppliers, the store was able to get both suppliers to co-op the same commercials. Their total budget was $7,000. But they were able to recover over $7,300 in co-op by advertising White-Westinghouse gas appliances.

Bonus Spots

Sometimes, instead of lowering the cost of the spots, you can get what the station calls bonus spots. These are freebies given to a client for advertising on their station. Though it's not exactly kosher, if your relationship with the reps is good, you can get them to put the bonus spots on a separate contract. That means, of course, that you don't have to advertise those products that are required to claim the co-op.

It might be to your advantage to pay rate card for your regular co-op spots, then use the bonus spots for those items that you can't co-op, like your service department. Of course, the true-blue diehards may frown upon this practice. Whether or not you should do it is a decision you'll have to make for yourself.

Procrastination Buying

Most stations close the log for Friday by 4:00 P.M. on Wednesday. So if you have some extra money lying around that you're just dying to spend on TV, give your rep a call on Wednesday at about 2:15 P.M. Tell him or her that you're considering placing $500 for this Friday, provided you can get a good deal. They'll scramble their little behinds off trying to set up all kinds of deals with the sales manager. (It's time that would have gone for public service announcements or station promotional spots.) If they can make a buck on it, there's a good chance you'll get a bargain. If they have no bargains, save the money for a rainy day.

Opportunity Program Buying

Once in a while you'll be fortunate enough to get a great deal of extra mileage out of a very few commercials. This is done with a technique that we've termed "opportunity program buying." It happened like this: A few years ago the then resident guru of health foods, the late Adele Davis, appeared on "The Merv Griffin Show." An alert TV sales rep approached a local health food shop and sold them four spots in the 90-minute show. Their business doubled!

By taking advantage of a show that features your product or service, you make a tremendous impact with your ads. You don't need to create a demand with your advertising, as is normally required, because the show will do that for you. The only thing you need to do is let the audience know where they can buy the product.

Seeing your type of product or service on a show has the same impact we mentioned earlier in the publicity chapter. People don't perceive the show as a commercial, so more people watch and pay much closer attention.

When Mary McFaden, nationally recognized sewing expert, appeared on "Phil Donahue," a fabric and yard shop bought four commercials that generated a number of responses.

When time is bought in a specific show like the two examples mentioned, it's wise to buy one spot in each commercial break. First, it will help you get the most out of the program. But most important, once a station sells you a spot in a commercial break, they don't sell a spot to a competitor in that same break. That knocks them out automatically.

A camera crew invaded the Nautilus Fitness Center to tape footage for a local newscast. The alert manager found out when the feature was going to run and bought commercials in and around those particular time periods. Three spots were purchased, yet the impact from the news items on the early and late news made those three spots have the same impact as 30.

When a local karate school found out that "Wide World of Sports" was going to show full-contact karate or other martial arts, one or two spots is all it took to see some results.

It is not often that one to four commercials in a flight will create much action for you. But if you can tie those commercials in with a show that effectively sells the product or service for you, it can work especially well. It's also a good time to use 10-second spots.

Finding out about opportunity programs is the difficult part. It takes an eager sales rep to keep an eye on the advance program booking sheets to find out which shows will have features that can do you some good. Another good point about this approach is that many of these shows are syndicated or on during not-the-best time periods. That means that you can buy the spots relatively inexpensively.

This approach may not work for every type of business. Usually, the narrower the target audience, the better off you are with this approach. But that's not always the case. Consider when CBS filmed Kenny Rogers in concert at the Wisconsin State Fair. The next morning a streetfighter in Madison, Wisconsin, purchased two spots in the show on the hunch many of the people that attended the concert would be watching just because it was filmed in their home town. His hunch was right. The ratings for that show, which aired many months later in Madison, went through the roof.

Another aspect of opportunity program-buying is to buy a show, even a fictional show, where the subject matter is related to your product or service. It always made sense to us that if you're a travel agency trying to sell a cruise, a show like "Love Boat" would be a natural. Trips to Vegas might do well on "Vegas," if it were still on the air. Private detective companies have many shows to choose from, but probably the most effective would be the afternoon soaps, which would give one more reason to enlist their services. Dance or music lessons might receive a little more attention from the audience of a show like "Fame." And companies specializing in very tall privacy fences might benefit greatly by advertising on "Leave It to Beaver" and "Dennis the Menace" reruns.

Lights, Action, Camera

Unlike radio stations, the TV stations have to charge for producing a TV spot. Your commercial can be as simple as three or four slides with their booth announcer. In such cases there is often no charge for the voice, just the photography. But if you want to get fancy, you have to pay for studio time, mini-cam time, editing, and some special effects.

Fill in the Hole

If you're going to the expense of making a decent TV spot, it is best to make it so you can get the most mileage out of it. For any special effects that have to be done at a great cost, like animation or slow motion, try to do them so that footage can be used repeatedly. For example, if you want to spend money on animation, we would recommend that you don't animate an individual spot, but rather use five-second tags at the end. An animated logo can be used indefinitely and can fit at the end of all spots you produce.

A good way to make the most efficient use of production time is to develop a good "donut." This is where you have a well-produced beginning and end and you merely fill in the holes with the products you want to feature. The center of the spot can be inexpensive slides or footage provided by your suppliers. And, of course, the donut contains all the vital information—your name, address, location, payment plans, and so on.

Once you book studio time, whether it's at a TV station or at an independent studio, it's going to cost you money for every minute you're in there, whether you get what you want or not. There are usually a few more problems in dealing with TV stations because they often have to break to cut into a commercial or to get ready for the local news. Yet, TV stations are usually less expensive than independent studios.

Your director is generally pretty conscientious. He or she wants to make you happy. But, the people who can kill you are the sound people, camera people, and others in the studio. Often they belong to a union and couldn't care less about your spot. If they mess up a shot, big deal—it doesn't cost them anything. So one thing we like to do just before we're ready to shoot a spot is to announce to the entire crew that if we get it on the first try ... the beer is on us. That really gets their attention and really cuts down the camera shaking accidentally or the sound person missing a cue. It could save you hundreds of dollars in studio time, and if you look for a sale, you could probably pick up a case of Old Milwaukee for seven or eight bucks. What a great return on investment.

Mini-cam works much the same way. This is a portable camera that's brought out to your store, the film to be edited later. The charge is by the hour. Most rate cards we've dealt with allowed a premium for the first hour with a little break for each hour thereafter. But, if you run 15 minutes into the next hour, you pay for the entire hour.

After each shoot on location, the camera person always goes to lunch with us. You'd be surprised how many partial hours are forgotten about after a $7 lunch. Why on one occasion, the camera man was treated to a nice $10 lunch and he forgot about the entire session altogether.

Keep in mind that these production people are on salary. They work very hard and are seldom shown signs of appreciation. A lunch here or a drink there can really go a long way not only in keeping production costs down, but in establishing a good relationship with these people. Then, when you need a favor or have an emergency spot to do, you stand a much greater chance of getting their cooperation.

The Spot that Got Censored

Fort Wayne is a conservative community (often referred to as the city of churches). But we have our share of "adult" bookstores, X-rated movie houses, and strip bars. Our client, Brickley's Firehouse, decided, as a novelty, to have male strippers for women only on a Monday night. They weren't usually even open on Monday, since business is slow then. But this feature was seeing a great deal of success in other markets and they wanted to try it in Fort Wayne.

The target audience for this event is quite different from their normal crowd. Married women, predominantly housewives, we were told, would make up the majority of the audience. The most efficient way to reach that group is with daytime soaps on TV. So we ordered the time and scheduled production.

There was a slight problem in putting the spot together—we had nothing to work with. No picture of our headliner, no footage, no nothing. We came up with an idea that dealt with this problem. The spot was shot in less than half an hour and edited in another half hour. The total cost of production was a little over $100 and it made such an impact that it was jerked off the station the second time it ran.

What was it? Well, we didn't think it was so bad. It opens with a shot of a man's chest. He's buttoning up his shirt. The announcer says, "This is Turk Johnson getting dressed to go to Brickley's Firehouse to get undressed for you this Monday." Then the announcer goes on to tell all of Turk's qualifications, which include an appearance on "Phil Donahue," and winning Mr. Nude America one year. While this narrative is going on, the spot shows different angles of our actor, never revealing his face, of course. One angle is a close-up of him putting on a ring, another is a side shot of him zipping up his Levis. Don't get excited, because you can't see a thing—he's just pulling up a zipper, no big deal.

Needless to say, somebody thought it *was* a big deal, and the station got a nasty phone call from a viewer about the spot, so they pulled it off the air. What really upset us was that the spot was probably the most prudish thing on the air. The station breaks during a soap that shows two people between the sheets giving a performance that looks as if it would register at least three points on the Richter scale. Then a commercial pops on for some kind of tampon, immediately followed by a spot for a douche. Then our bland spot for Turk Johnson hits the air, followed by a scented minipad commercial and a Donahue promotion for tomorrow's show on human sexuality. Then it's back to the couple in bed doing their imitation of the Mount St. Helen's eruption.

There's no justice in the world, well at least not in Fort Wayne. When our spot was censored, we had to delete the infamous zipper scene before they would let us put it on the air again. The promotion was approaching rapidly so we had no choice. Out came the zipper. It was replaced with some footage of shoe tying. While this was not exactly the effect we had in mind, the promotion was a big success.

The important point is twofold: One, you don't have to spend a fortune to get an effective piece of production; the set was black, no background; there was one person, with little action. Two, know what the station will allow on the air.

Ask for the Order

One of the biggest problems with many local TV spots is they don't ask for the order. You have to tell people to buy, visit, or call. You have to give them an action to do or they won't do it. On a limited budget, forget institutional advertising. You can't afford it, and it's hard to track results. Advertise with the intention of selling something.

Put It in Writing

In your production emphasize the key point of the copy or script with "lower-third supers." These are the words on the bottom of the screen over the regular video. Don't confuse the audience by putting up supers that tell something completely different from what the audio portion is telling them. Chances are they'll get so confused they'll forget both messages. If your announcer is saying, "Save $20," that should also appear on the screen. It's done with a "character generator." It costs little or nothing and really helps to reinforce the message of your spot. People have a tendency to remember what they read *and* hear more than if they just read it or just hear it.

A Star Is Torn

A good way to get attention in your spot is with a recognizable spokesperson. Ed McMahon goes out for about $20,000 a pop. You can pick up Bill Cosby for a little less. Or you can look around for someone in your city who might serve that purpose.

We lucked out—probably won't happen again in our lifetime, but we pulled this one off and it's worth sharing. A lawn and garden client needed something to make his spots a little more memorable. He liked doing his own spots but didn't give the strongest delivery. By some stroke of luck we were able to get one of the affiliate stations to let us use their sportscaster as our spokesperson.

They never, never, never let any of their newspeople represent a business because they feel it challenges their credibility. They're probably right, but it never hurts to ask. As it turned out, this sportscaster was without a doubt the most popular one in the city. He was also a good friend of ours. We knew that his contract was up for renewal. The station didn't want to pay him any more money but they couldn't afford to lose him because his ratings were very good. They also knew that our client wasn't buying any time on that station. With all of these factors together, they conceded to let us use him as our client's spokesperson, provided that we shift our TV budget to their station. That only made sense anyway, for the same reason that opportunity program-buying works.

An entire campaign was developed centering around this sportscaster using a sports theme. Since they were selling heavy garden equipment and the majority of their customers were men, everything seemed to fall into place. For an annual retainer of only $750, we shot six spots. In addition, we set up a special deal with a radio station: The sportscaster would do a five-minute call-in show once a day during afternoon drive time. Our client cosponsored that, and the radio station paid the sportscaster. Part of the deal we negotiated was that at the end of the show, the radio station would plug the sportscaster's newscast on TV. The TV station went along with that. The last thing we were able to set up was to get our celebrity to write a weekly article in the local cable magazine. Again, the client sponsored part of that and the magazine paid the sportscaster for the article, plus plugged his TV show.

It was the classic everyone-wins situation. The garden shop received the use of a powerful local figure at a very reasonable rate. (Part of the deal was that we handle the sportcaster's personal PR, which we did.) The radio and magazine exposure was good for the TV show and for our celebrity, plus, all the outside activities made him enough extra money to keep him happy for awhile.

The spots were set up like a sports interview in which the owner was interviewed by the sports personality. After some time, the owner was associated with the sportscaster, enough that he became a local celebrity in his own right, which was very important. You see, after all of the wheeling and dealing we did for this sportscaster, he got enough impact to get an offer from a major market.

No doubt, we fell into it. But at least we weren't afraid to ask. You have to know what the motivations are of each person you're trying to work with. Knowing this, you can then appeal to them on terms that will motivate them to action. The same expertise you use to sell your own customers needs to be used when trying to sell a TV sales representative, traffic department head, station manager, or even a local celebrity.

Make Yourself a Star

Don't laugh. Doing your own commercials can be very effective. Lee Iacocca found that out. On a local level you can become a celebrity in your own right using TV advertising. When people come to your store, they'll recognize you. They'll be in awe of you. They'll want to buy whatever you recommend. You are a celebrity.

Sure, it's a nice ego trip. But ego aside, if you can speak half-way clearly, consider doing your own spots. You don't have to come across as the polished announcer type. As a matter of fact, if you did, it wouldn't have the impact.

Even boring spots work when done by the owner, as evidenced by a car dealership. This owner appeared in his own commercials for years. It was probably the most boring presentation you'd ever want to cry through, but it was credible. The interesting thing about it was that when one of his salespeople was having a little trouble closing a prospect, he would come to the rescue. He was a celebrity. Customers wanted to shake his hand. They also wanted to buy his product because if someone as important as he would take the time to talk to a lowly customer, they should be honored.

The Tale of the Tube

TV is powerful, no doubt about it. How long it will work is anyone's guess. Look out for new developments in cable, and if you're using TV, try to track the results to see if it's still working for you.

If you're just using TV for the first time, approach with extreme caution. Make sure you load everything in your favor.

And the next time you're going to the bathroom during a commercial, just think to yourself how much that merchant paid to reach you—maybe that's why they put that little man in the rowboat floating in the toilet.

9

PRINT:
LINING BIRD CAGES
AND TRAINING PUPPIES

"Extra! Extra! Read all about it." The only time you see a newsboy on a street corner yelling that anymore is in the movies, and usually it's in black and white. Newspapers were among the first mass advertising media, but times have changed. It still works for small retailers with small budgets, but as we say all too often, not as well as it once did.

Take a long hard look at those circulation figures. How much of it is from readers outside your city? How much of your business is from outside the city? You may have noticed something else about the circulation figures. They're getting smaller. But despite a rapid decline in the readership of daily newspapers, the prices continue to soar.

Of course, sometimes the prices don't go up; the size of the ads is reduced. This is how some papers avoid having a price increase. They'll add another column to the paper, which in effect is a price hike, since you'd have to pay more to get the same size ad as before.

Another thing that's changing rapidly with newspapers is that there are fast becoming fewer of them. Major dailies are going belly-up, leaving the only survivor in a very strong position.

Newspapers are monopolies. They don't negotiate price opposition. They've never heard the meaning of the words "make-good." If they make a mistake in your full-page ad, they'll rerun just the portion that was in error. It might be a minor problem, such as forgetting your logo, address, or phone number. Even so, your make-good will consist of a two-column by two-inch ad. And the rest of the full page? Well, that's just too bad.

Why should they worry? After all, where else can you go? You're stuck with them. And newspaper can still work if it's done right. Even though we are somewhat limited as to what we can do in a streetfighting sense with newspaper, we still have a few tricks up our sleeves. So if we make it sound like newspaper is good only for lining bird cages and training puppies, don't believe it. There are many other uses for newspaper, such as starting firewood, wrapping fish, and yes, even advertising.

The Streetfighter's Cheater Page

Do you ever run a full-page ad? Perhaps during one of your major sales or promotions you use a full page. It definitely makes a big impact, no doubt about it. But next time you're going to place a full-page ad, use what we call a "streetfighter's cheater page." In this, your ad is three or four inches from the top of the page and one column less than full. You shouldn't lose any readership from this. Yet you'll save quite a bit of money over the full page, since the paper charges by the total amount of space you use.

As a matter of fact, you might even pick up some additional readership because you stand a decent chance of getting some editorial copy in the extra space you left behind. So while a reader might have just passed you by if your page was all advertising, you shave a shot at getting that person reading those small articles.

You'll still be the dominant ad on the page. The only other ads they could possibly put next to you would be ads that are only one column wide.

Position is very important, too. All things being equal, you should get better readership if your ad is on the right side above the center line. Now there's no way to guarantee position. As a matter of fact, the paper will want to charge you some obscene fee for a special position. Usually, that extra cost doesn't justify doing it.

One way to make sure your ad does go above center line is to produce an ad that's three or four inches taller than half the size of the paper. Simple enough. By doing this, you ensure that readers will be able to see your headline even when the paper is folded.

If you wish to totally dominate the page, you can do it without buying the entire page or even a cheater page for that matter. All you need to do is have your ad three or four inches above the center line and one column wider than half the width of the paper. If your paper is nine columns wide, for example, your ad needs to be five columns wide.

There's no way another ad on that page could be any bigger than yours, yet you pay almost a third of a full-page ad rate.

The real art of newspaper advertising is determining the smallest ad you can get away with and still get the results you want. The smaller the ad, the less the cost. That allows you more money in other areas like TV, radio, or even the bottom line. Each business is different. You'll have to test and track; try to get a feeling for the size ads that show the biggest return on investment.

A study done a number of years ago indicated that a two-thirds page ad got about 11 percent readership. When that ad was cut down to one-third of a page, the readership was 8 percent. That's a loss of 3-percent readership, but the price was half. So if you can determine the point of diminishing returns in the size of your newspaper ad, you could save a bunch of money.

Multimedia Mixing

When running a big sale or promotion for which you're using newspaper with TV or radio support, it helps to cross-reference the print ad in your broadcast ad. Your TV or radio spot gives you just enough time for creating awareness of the sale and maybe listing one or two examples. Your newspaper ad, on the other hand, will allow you to provide a list of more products with more complete descriptions. So in your broadcast spots tell the audience to look for your ad in tomorrow morning's newspaper. The same technique works for direct mail campaigns as well.

Then turn around in your newspaper ad and cross-reference your products that were in the broadcast spots with AS SEEN ON TV. Also, make sure that all your ads, regardless of the medium, have continuity. The name of the sale used in the paper should be the same name used on radio or TV. It sounds like common sense, but you'd be surprised how many merchants don't do it. Getting your mass media advertising to work together can help you create a better response than if they're separate elements.

Coming Out of His Shell

There's an interesting example of a merchant in Arizona who was really able to cash in on tying his newspaper ad to TV. He was selling a novelty called "pearls in the oyster." You could buy a pearl, still in the oyster, and have it mounted in a necklace or whatever you wanted. It was a nice little gimmick and made them some money. All of the sudden, another company started selling the same item on TV through an 800 toll-free number.

At first he panicked. But after he gave it some thought, he began to use newspaper advertising. In his ad in big letters was "AS SEEN ON TV." He then undercut the TV offer by a buck and stressed that his customers could pick their pearls up right away instead of waiting to get them through the mail. The competition's TV ad probably helped him in the long run.

The Teaser Technique

For those facing a very small budget, half-page ads are out of the question. So why not try the teaser ad? This is a very small ad, could be one column by one to four inches tall. They're spread throughout the paper, maybe three, four, or five times. The ads themselves won't generate a tremendous amount of impact. But, with the frequency you'll get, you can make them very memorable.

One of our favorite examples of a newspaper teaser ad was used by Jeff when he was a junior attending Indiana University in Bloomington—famous for Crest Toothpaste and the Kinsey Sex Clinic (the University, not Jeff). He was elected to the Union Board of Directors (a group of a dozen students in charge of providing various programs for the student body). Jeff's area was theater.

He wasn't happy putting on just any show—no way. He wrote his own show entitled *Sinner On The Roof*. It was a musical parody using the original musical score from *Fiddler On The Roof*. His version was a colorful story about life on a large college campus as seen through the eyes of freshmen. It included such immortal hits as "Dope Pusher, Dope Pusher" to the tune of "Match Maker, Match Maker," and "Throw Up, Fall Down" to the tune of "Sunrise, Sunset," to name a few.

Jeff's responsibility, other than writing this show, was producing it. This was probably his first practical use of streetfighting as we know it today. The school newspaper was well read by the students and was the obvious place to advertise. But the student production's promotional budget was very small. As a result, the ads were, too. So, a teaser campaign was done.

Now keep in mind that while this show may offend the average mortal, it was written and performed by students. Understanding his target audience (being one himself) Jeff placed a number of one-column by three-inch ads. The headline in one read DOPE with a subhead of "Just one of the things you'll see in *Sinner On The Roof.*" Then there was a line for the times and location of the show. Another read BOOZE, and the last read SEX.

Those small ads received a great deal of attention. In addition to the campus newspaper, fliers and posters were used. Again, thinking of that target audience and how to best reach them, this is what he did. The majority of the students lived in the dorms. In the dorm you don't have your own bathroom, you share a large one that will accommodate everyone on your dorm floor (anywhere from 50 to 100 students). To get 100 percent penetration of the dorms, posters for the play were placed in front of every toilet and urinal in all the dorm buildings. One person would handle an entire building in less than an hour. A committee of 12 covered the entire campus, reaching close to 20,000 students in less than one day. Very efficient. And besides, you have a captive audience, unless of course they bring the paper in with them to read. (But, he would get them there, too, with the newspaper ads.)

One other little technique that he used to get the word out about the play was out of the ordinary. Though it doesn't relate to print advertising, it still is worth mentioning. Two people on the theater committee would sit on opposite sides of the cafeteria in the dorm. There might be as many as 300 to 400 people eating there at any one time.

All of a sudden one person would stand up and yell to his friend on the other side (at the top of his lungs), "Hey John."

"Hi Joe, what's up?"

"Are you going to *Sinner On The Roof?*"

"When is it?"
"This Friday and Saturday at Alumni Hall."
"Sure, I'll go."

Half the crowd would follow the conversation between these two. As one would start yelling to the other, the audience would turn their heads. It looked like the audience at a tennis match. But the point is, it created awareness for the show and it didn't cost anything to do it. And while the show didn't sell out, there was a good crowd at all four performances, with a standing ovation at the last one.

Bad Printing

Since we're on the subject of college, there was one very interesting story that does have to do with the newspaper. About once a semester, during a special promotion for the students, the Union Board would sponsor a free movie program. All you had to do was show your student ID and you could get in free. Very popular promotion. But one year had a better turnout than all the others.

The student advertising director prepared a very nice-looking ad for the newspaper announcing the promotions. The headline read FREE FLICKS. He used a very tall, thin, block type style with the letters very close together. It was elegant. Had the ad run in a magazine in which the printing is of much greater quality than that of a newspaper, there probably wouldn't have been any problem. But when the paper reproduced the ad on newsprint, the *L* and the *I* in the word FLICKS ran together to form a *U*.

No one seemed disappointed when they came to the auditorium and all they could get was a free movie. However, the faculty advisor conducted a brief investigation. The ad director acted totally dumb-founded and couldn't figure out how it could happen—but then, he was getting his minor in drama.

Black and White

To get the most attention from a particularly small space ad, the proper use of white space and black space is very helpful. First, don't try to cram too much copy in too small an area. Give it some air.

Otherwise the ad will look too cramped and confused. The reader will be turned off.

The use of black space, or a *reverse,* is good for headlines. This is white letters on a black background. You don't want the entire ad like that, especially the body copy, because it would be more difficult to read and makes the ad look dirty. But for a simple headline, that big patch of black really grabs the eye.

Also, if you let the newspaper set the type and paste up the ad for you, you might want to keep in mind that as a rule their idea of creativity is using a dozen different type styles in the same ad. They might do it out of sheer boredom or trying to be creative, but it makes your ad look too confusing. When sending copy to the paper put the following disclaimer on it:

> Set all copy in Futura, Helvetica, or comparable sans serif typeface. Use no italics. Use bold only where indicated.

Never mind what it means—it's just a bunch of technical jargon that the paper will understand. All you need to know is that by putting those instructions with your ad copy, your ad should come out looking pretty clean.

Headlines

Short and bold. If you're running a sale, put the word "SALE!" in three-inch letters at the top. Other attention-getters might be: CLEARANCE!, SAVE!, FREE!, HALF OFF!, or DEALS!. Keep it brief.

Body Copy

It's best to tell people how much they're going to save in dollars, not percentages. "Save 25%" doesn't have the impact that "Save $12" does. People don't think in percentages unless you're advertising to bookies or meteorologists.

Write the way you talk. Use contractions and simple words. Don't tell people to *masticate* when you want them to *chew.* Words that seem to get attention in print advertising are *Discover, Free, Easy, Health, You, Save, Sale, Guarantee, Proven, Money, New,* and *Love.*

Those twelve words have been used for years, over and over again. Perhaps overused, yet they still seem to get the readers' attention. Then there are the fad words. Words that get attention for a certain period. Words like *Natural, Organic,* and *Light* or *Lite.* It seems as soon as there's a reasonably successful product on the market, they water it down a little and introduce the light version. Maybe in the second edition of this book we can edit it so there's one-third fewer pages and call it *Streetfighting Light.*

Choose your words carefully. Make sure they fit your products and services. Don't waste precious ad space on copy that doesn't sell or doesn't keep your readers' interest.

What's in It for Me?

Stress the *you* benefits. Don't talk about we. One of our newsletter readers was once very excited about learning these words that could help her put more punch in her advertising copy. So enthusiastic, in fact, that she came up with the line: "Discover the Free and Easy way You are Guaranteed to Love our New Proven Money Saving Sale!" The only word she forgot was "health," which was too bad because one of the items she was selling was vitamins.

Nobody cares about we. They want to know what's in it for them. Just because you've been in business for 50 years is not reason enough for them to shop you. Give them a reason why your being in business 50 years is a benefit to them.

Use short sentences. Simple. Brief. People don't talk in sentences. They talk in phrases. Write that way. Easy to read. Easy to understand.

Last, ask for the order. Buy now. Visit today. Call us soon. Don't delay. Tell them to take some kind of specific action.

You might get a little more attention with broken borders even if you don't use coupons. In today's economy people are very sensitive to coupons, and a broken border will catch their attention. If you're going to use a coupon, don't tell them to bring this ad in for the discount. Print an actual coupon with a broken border. Greater impact. Place that coupon in your ad so it's easy to cut out. Put it near a corner or an edge. But, better yet, don't put a coupon in your ad at all. Save that for cross-promotions. Protect your regular price credibility. There's no way to transfer the responsibility for the discount in a newspaper ad.

Which Contract You Should Sign

There are two different strategies you could use when it comes to signing a lineage contract. In most papers, the more column inches, lines, or whatever they use to determine the size of an ad, the less it costs per unit. The open rate may be $10 a column inch for example. If you sign a contract that states you'll buy at least 1,000 inches that year, the rate may drop to $9.25. At 2,500 inches, it may drop to $8.90, and so on.

If you sign a contract and don't buy as much as the contract calls for, they will not confiscate your first-born male child. They'll short rate you. That means you'll receive a bill at the end of the year that makes up the difference between what you actually paid and what you should have paid based on the amount of space you used.

On the other hand, if you used more than the contract called for and that additional space would have entitled you to a break in the price, they'll usually issue you a credit or refund.

If you're paying for the space yourself, that is, without co-op funds, then you might consider signing the largest contract you can. That means you'll be paying less all year. Of course, you'll get a bill at the end of the year demanding the difference, but you got to use their money all that time, interest free.

If you use co-op funds, that's a different story. Your co-op source will pay you based on the gross amount of the newspaper invoice. Therefore, you should sign the smallest contract you can. In doing so you'll by paying a much higher rate all year long, which means your co-op source will be reimbursing you at that higher rate. Then at the end of the year you'll be issued a credit or refund.

The Free Classified Ad

As you can probably tell, we get frustrated dealing with newspapers. But there are times when you have to use them. So we put on our Miss America smile and try to make the best of it. It's just that some order-takers at the newspaper are so hard to deal with. Notice we said order-takers, not salespeople.

Mostly out of frustration, or just to see if it would work, we did a little something that got us a little bit of free exposure (not a lot). We were at the paper placing a classified ad when we noticed they had an ongoing promotion for free "found" ads. If you found a lost dog, you could place an ad in both papers for three days (up to three lines) for nothing.

The price was right. All we had to do was find something. We told the clerk that we found a three-ring binder with eight copies of the *Streetfighter* newsletter (see Figure 9-1). We gave her our office number. An item appeared in both papers for three days. It was a mention, and of course nobody called to claim it.

Figure 9-1

It probably wasn't worth a special trip to the paper to do it. But since we were there, why not? A few weeks after that ad appeared, we placed another. This time it was for a client of ours (see Figure 9-2). Not only did we get their name mentioned, but their location as well.

Nobody called for this one either.

Figure 9-2

Tabloids, Shoppers, and Pennysavers

They're cropping up all over the place and can be an alternative to some newspaper advertising. Some work, some don't. Some work well. The only thing we can tell you to do is test and track.

One thing that we have noticed with some regularity is that the front cover generally works very well. At the very least you can make a general impression while it's on the way to the waste basket. It also seems to work better in two colors.

But many other people have discovered the same thing. In some areas you may find that the front cover is booked for months or even years in advance. We had one client whose local tabloid was booked five years in advance. In such cases, get your name on their waiting list. And you'd best have a camera-ready ad on the shelf ready to go on a moment's notice.

Tabloids are more negotiable than newspapers. They'll trade and even dicker over the price. Other areas of negotiation might be a second color free, or a first right of refusal if there's a cancellation.

To compare the results from a tabloid versus a newspaper, run a coupon in each. Use the same offer. Then track the results of the number of coupons redeemed. Divide the number redeemed into the cost of the ad. The lowest number wins. Don't be surprised if the tabloids give you more redemptions at a fourth of the cost. It's happened before.

Magazines

Any local magazine is another medium you'll just have to test and track. In markets where cable penetration is very high, a cable guide magazine might be very beneficial. But you should also see how detailed the cable listings are in the paper.

Local monthly magazines is a judgment call on your part. If it's something that's given to each person staying in local hotels, and your business is such that it attracts a great number of tourists, maybe you should consider it. On the other hand, watch the method of distribution very carefully. If they're just laid out on a table each month where the employees glance through them and then dump them, you might think twice. Ask how the magazine comes by their circulation figures.

Let Your Fingers Do the Talking

Yellow Pages. Probably the best-trained sales staff in any of the media. These people are good. Be careful.

Will it work for you? Depends on your type of business. Yellow Pages are very expensive. And you're stuck with it for the entire year whether you like it or not.

Any type of service business probably should be strong in the Yellow Pages. Businesses that people call to have something done like fix your TV or tow your car away should be in Yellow Pages. Any kind of service that consumers don't need every day should also be in the Yellow Pages. They will look for your company when there's a problem.

Businesses that depend on a high amount of foot traffic or that sell common items that people use every day probably could get by without too much in the Yellow Pages. Most people won't look in the Yellow Pages to go to a restaurant. They'll look in the entertainment section of the newspaper. Try to get into the consumer's mind and see how you would react in his or her position.

An ad in the Yellow Pages should be the one ad above all for which you seek professional help. With as much as you're going to pay for it, and since you're stuck with it all year, get a good ad agency or an independent layout artist to help you with it. It'll be money well spent.

If you need some ideas on what to put in your Yellow Pages ad, go to the public library. There you'll find telephone books for most major cities in the country. See what like businesses are doing for their Yellow Pages ads. It's a great way to get some good ideas.

If you ever need to come up with a name for a new business, keep that same technique in mind. You can get some great ideas from those Yellow Pages, and it's all free. Just make sure you don't try to steal (creatively borrow) a name that's been copyrighted.

Boldface Listings in White Pages

It's different for every business. When people are looking in the white pages, they already know your name. So if your name is unique, you can get by without a boldface listing. But if your name also contains your product, and your competitor's does too, you probably should have it in bold. For example, Pizza Hut and Pizza Inn would be located very close to each other. Anybody looking up one in the white pages will probably see both, and there will be a battle to see who gets the order.

On the other hand, Godfather's Pizza will be listed all by itself with no other pizza competition on the page.

Don't Mention It

As mentioned earlier, it's usually a good idea to cross-reference your advertising among media. The exception to this is the Yellow Pages.

Merchants will often tell readers, viewers, or listeners, to look for their ad in the Yellow Pages. Dumb. By doing that you're inviting that prospect to also call each and every one of your competitors. They're all right there on the same page. Even if your ad dominates that page, you have a number of your competitors right there too. It's too easy for readers to get sidetracked. If you want them to learn more about what you have to offer, have them call or write you.

The same thing goes for those stickers you put on your store window and delivery vehicles. It's just inviting people to comparison shop.

Yellow Pages ads should stand on their own merit. If you have to cross-reference them to make them work, you should seriously consider a size reduction. Remember, you're not advertising a sale in the Yellow Pages like you would be in a newspaper ad. Plus, in the newspaper you should not be right next to your competitor unless, of course, you're in classified.

Yellow Pages Alternatives

Competition is springing up all over the country for Yellow Pages. It's usually very well received by the merchants because most merchants don't like dealing with Yellow Pages. Do they work? We've heard mixed reports. Again, it's a matter of testing and tracking results.

While this competition does keep the Yellow Pages from having a monopoly, it also makes your directory decision more complicated. Should you be in both? If so, what size ad in each? And with two books, you have to spend much more money. Not only that, but which book will people use the most? So while the Yellow Pages people might be humbled to some degree, there's another problem: the watering-down effect caused by too many phone books.

Community Directories

Adding to the watering-down effect are the small community versions of the phone book complete with Yellow Pages. So you might need to advertise in the regular Yellow Pages to the entire metropolitan area, plus take out an ad in the alternative Yellow Pages, and still have to consider the effect of using these community editions. Each community is different. Do your customers use the major phone directory or the smaller community version?

If you had to make a choice between the two, you probably could do without the community Yellow Pages. We only say that because it's hard to get people to break old habits. They've been using the big phone book for a long time and the smaller version might not have all the listings they need. As always, it's a judgment call on your part.

When possible, take out the smallest ad in the Yellow Pages that you feel you can get away with, unless you're absolutely sure that your ad is showing you a good return on investment.

Tracking results of all forms of advertising will be discussed in the last chapter, so hang on.

City Directory
What a waste. Forget it.

Bowling Score Sheets
Forget it.

High School Program Ads
If you don't know about this by now, reread chapter three on community involvement. (Hint: In most cases, forget it.)

Competitive Exit

What happens if a competitor goes down the tubes? How can you get as many of their customers as possible? One merchant did it this way. When a business went under, he had the phone company install a phone with their old number at his business. So whenever anyone would call to order from them, he would tell them, "That particular company is no longer with us, but we'll be glad to help you." He got the benefit of their loyal customer base as well as their listings in both the white pages and Yellow Pages for the remainder of the year. Great move.

10

THE GREAT OUTDOORS!
IS IT REALLY SO GREAT?

For retail merchants, outdoor advertising might not be all that great. As a matter of fact, if it weren't for cigarettes, liquor, radio stations, and an occasional politician, the billboard companies might be in a footrace for Chapter 11 papers.

It's not that billboard advertising doesn't pull in business for retailers, though we have our doubts, it's just that it's so expensive. But even so, there are some good uses of billboards and ways of getting the most out of them.

Paper Posting

The most common billboard is the "30-sheet posting." This is a billboard on which paper is pasted up to fill the board with the message, as opposed to a painted board, which is usually bigger and painted directly on wood panels.

Grossly Overrated

Billboard companies prefer to sell you a showing of a number of boards at one time, which they designate as a GRP showing. GRP stands for Gross Rating Points, and they have all kinds of elaborate mathematics that tell how many people see the board during the course of the month.

The GRPs are presented in multiples of 25. For example, a 25 GRP showing in a given city might include a total of five boards, four of which are lighted. In a 200 GRP showing, you would receive 40 boards. While GRPs stand for a rating system, it's pretty worthless, so don't get confused by billboard company jargon. The GRPs are meaningless. Only two things really matter: How many boards you get for your money, and where these boards are located.

Though you're alloted so many boards for a given GRP showing, they usually don't designate exactly where those boards will be. A board in a high-traffic area will obviously deliver a larger viewership than a board at a low-traffic area, even though both boards may sell for the same amount of money. And that's your point of negotiation. While they won't come down on the price in most instances, you can negotiate high-traffic locations that will get you the largest viewership for the dollar.

The Every-Other-Month Strategy

Thirty-sheet postings are sold by the month. If you're convinced that billboards are the way for your business to advertise, then you probably have signed an annual contract for your boards. There is a way to get the effect of a full year at a price slightly more than half of what that year would cost. Alternate months for a year. One month you're up, the next you're not. You'll by paying for six months, but many of the boards will remain up much longer than the 30 days. Some may never come down, because if the billboard company doesn't have a client to replace it right away, it just costs them extra money to rip it down.

It is somewhat of a gamble, and there's no way to know for sure just how much free time you'll get. It works best in the northern states, especially around the first of the year when the weather is miserable. Streetfighters in northern states might fare better with this strategy since no one would want to go outside to tear down a board when it's $10°$ below with wind chill factor of $40°$ below.

If you're going to put on a showing for just a month, you might try the same strategy with a two-week posting. A two-week posting costs 60 to 70 percent of a one-month. But again, with a little luck you can get a full month or better on some of those boards.

You could alternate months or two-week showings with half of your schedule should the thought of no exposure feel uncomfortable, and you order a fairly large showing. For example, five boards might be the smallest. So if you order ten boards, you can alternate each month between ten and five boards, then see how much free exposure you get on the off months. For two-week postings, you could take out five boards for an entire month, then at the beginning of the month, an additional five boards for two weeks. Then see how many extra days you get on the two-week boards.

When ordering production be sure to get enough paper to handle all of the boards you've ordered and a little extra. Sometimes a board might get ripped in bad weather and you don't want to have a half visible board up. Also, a few extra copies of the production make high-impact backdrops for booths at off-premises promotions.

Another service that few advertisers are aware of is masking. The eight panels of your board are slightly smaller than the actual billboard itself. So there will be an uneven white border around your ad, provided, of course, your background color isn't white. For a few bucks a board, you can get matching strips of paper, the same color as your background color. This will make your board appear slightly bigger than most of the other ones. Works great when your board is competing with a couple of others.

Spikes and Snipe

Ever gone snipe hunting? If you're looking for snipe, you'll find them on billboards. *Snipe* or *spikes* are strips that can be pasted over your regular board. This is nice with multilocations because you don't have to change the actual production for each location if you want to give the address of the one nearest that board. You simply have the address line printed on strips of paper that appear at the bottom of the board.

Other uses of spikes are to make announcements. You've been having a moving sale for a month. The last week you might put up a spike across the board that says Ending Soon or Final Week. This adds immediacy to the campaign, and the change in the board should attract a little more attention.

Perhaps the most creative use of a spike was used by a politician. The election was over, yet he still had a week or so left on his board. So he had a spike put diagonally across the board that simply said, Thank You. Nice touch.

Which Way Did They Go?

Perhaps the best use of billboard for retail merchants is a directional. It's very important if your business is a little difficult to find, or just off a major thoroughfare. Again, keep the message simple. Use an arrow if possible and brief directions like: left at light, or next exit.

If you need a directional board and want only one of them, you'll have to pay a premium for it. No way around it in most cases. They really hate selling just one board, especially if it's one of their better locations. You'll just have to live with it.

Juniors: Hit or Miss

Junior billboards are the midget boards you see around town. They're fairly reasonable in price compared to regular billboards, but they're also much smaller. They'll work pretty good in a congested area like a downtown where much of the traffic is very slow pace and pedestrian.

Juniors can also be used to help increase your frequency of a regular billboard showing much in the same way 10-second TV spots are used to help the 30s. With juniors, however, you have to keep the message extremely brief, more so than the regular boards.

Ring Around the Rotary

Then there are the big boards. The huge boards. The mammoth boards. Some of the big boards move around. This is a rotary board. Every two months, they pack up their bags and move to a new location somewhere in town.

These boards are painted on vertical panels. You buy them for a year and get a two-month showing in six different locations. Very expensive. You probably could find a better use of your advertising money.

If you're going to use them, however, be sure to negotiate the six locations up front. Pick good ones or live with your choice the rest of the year.

Let There Be Light

On many boards, especially the large painted ones, there are lights. Before you sign a contract, find out exactly when the lights are turned on and off. During the winter especially, when it gets dark sooner, make sure the lights get turned on early so you catch all of the people driving home from work. What time the lights are turned on and off is also a good last-minute negotiation ploy. Try to get an extra hour in the evening on your boards. It could only help, and it doesn't cost anything to ask.

Renewing Contracts

If you use the same board again, you might want to wait to the very last minute to renew the contract. When you refuse to renew it months in advance, the billboard company has plenty of time to find a replacement. But by waiting until the very last minute, you can scare them half to death by hesitating. If for some reason you don't renew, they're stuck with no income from that board for a month or more until they find a replacement. At that point you'll be in a stronger negotiating position, since the loss of one month's revenue would be far greater than the little trifle you'll propose.

Lastly, when using painted boards, be sure to see how often the boards will be painted. They can get pretty ratty looking after a rough winter. That's also a last-minute negotiation point. Get an extra painting thrown in.

Marquee Facade

Movable signs like marquees, and portable readerboards, as tacky as you might think they are, are great for drumming up business. You have the flexibility of communicating with passersby on a daily basis. That message can change as often as you like. With the computerized boards you can change the message every other minute if you like, complete with graphics.

They work. If you don't have one, get one. People do read them. Think how much it would cost you to buy one billboard at your location each month. Many hundreds of dollars. The marquee or porta-sign is your own, and usually for not too much money.

Are You Open?

One of the first rules with readerboards is never leave the sign blank. It gives the impression that you're closed. Also, you should change the message at least once a week. In very high-traffic areas, where you get a lot of the same people passing by every day, you may want to consider changing it more often.

The owner of a grocery store in a small town in Ohio was not convinced that readerboards were all that great. After a great deal of convincing, he finally acquired one. The first thing he advertised was head lettuce at a certain price. He sold more lettuce that week than ever before. After that, whatever he advertised on his readerboard he would sell tons of. He soon became an avid believer in readerboards. So much so that he even strongly considered buying a $25,000 computerized board. Aside from the board itself, the electricity to run one was about $800 a month, so he just kept his regular board.

Trading Boards

Every readerboard has two sides. Provided you're not on a one-way street, both sides will be visible, but the people who will see your sign are probably the same ones day after day.

To expand your audience with your readerboard, find another merchant on a different street, preferably one that has as much traffic as yours, if not more. Then suggest that you trade one side of your board for one side of his. That way you both can reach a different group of people. A cross-promotion of porta-signs if you will.

A small improvement of that idea could get you exposure on another high-traffic area in town. Find a merchant with a very good location who doesn't have a readerboard. Then offer to place a board at his location, free. He gets one side, you get the other. The sides alternate weekly and the only cost for him is the electricity to light the board. Also, you might want to be responsible for changing your side of the board weekly if you think this merchant wouldn't do it right away. But, if he is very trustworthy, changing the board could be his responsibility, and all you would have to do is phone in your message.

Should you do this, be sure to get a contract drawn up that shows you own the board. You don't want any confusion there.

This technique can get you much exposure all over town at a relatively small cost. And once you have purchased the board, you own it and can use it over and over and over again.

A variation of this technique was used by an apartment complex. The manager approached the owners or managers of gas stations in his area at main intersections. He told them that people were having some difficulty finding his property and he would like to place a small directional sign in the grassy area near the street in front of the gas station. In return for that, he would have his maintenance crews cut their grass, free, all summer long.

He got about half-a-dozen of these signs up in this manner. Small signs about a-foot-and-a-half tall and about four feet long. Cut in the shape of an arrow pointing in the direction of his property. The message was simple, the name of the apartment complex. The signs were inexpensive to produce and once in the ground have remained for years.

Catch Me if You Ban

Many cities have ordinances banning the use of readerboards, and some have very strict rules on signage. A real problem.

There was a restaurant that sat off the main road so that if you didn't know it was there, you might miss it when you drove by. The manager wanted desperately to put a porta-sign at the edge of the parking lot near the road to draw some attention from passersby. Unfortunately, the city's elders passed an ordinance banning the use of portable readerboards. But there was a grandfather clause in the law. This allowed all those merchants who bought such signs prior to the banning to continue to use theirs. So there were still quite a few of these signs in use.

If there was some way to slip a sign in without anybody noticing, they might be able to keep it there for awhile. So the manager contacted the local Boy Scouts, who were looking for a place to sell Christmas trees. He volunteered the front half of his parking lot to this organization and their worthy cause. So sensitive was he to the importance of their program, that in his enthusiasm, he went out and bought a readerboard to help them advertise their Christmas tree sale.

He figured that no one in his right mind would prohibit the Boy Scouts from advertising their Christmas tree sale. He was right. And a month later, when the sale was over, the Boy Scouts left very happy, but the sign remained. As far as we know, it's still there today.

Say What?

You can use your boards to say whatever you want. Some use them for philosophical purposes, providing members of the community with bits and pieces of the proprietor's innermost thoughts. Many people look forward to reading these "people's" boards as a main source of entertainment. It couldn't be any worse than prime time television at any rate.

One of the more successful uses of a marquee was done by a Jeremiah Sweeny's franchisee in Lousiville, Kentucky. This is a fun restaurant—crazy decor, wild promotions. The owner was looking through the local phone book one day and chanced upon the name John Wayne. (This was back a few years when the Duke was still pushing Metamucil.) The owner called up Mr. Wayne and told him that his name was selected at random to have a free dinner for two. The night chosen for this event was Tuesday, not one of the hottest nights in the restaurant business.

On the readerboard outside of the restaurant, a message was placed: "John Wayne To Dine Here Soon." The message changed daily to build the excitement of the promotion. "John Wayne Will Dine Here Next Week." The enthusiasm was building rapidly as the message was changed to read, "John Wayne Will Dine Here This

Tuesday." Then, "John Wayne Will Dine Here Tomorrow." Finally, "John Wayne Will Dine Here Tonight at 8:00!"

The place was mobbed. Patrons packed in with their cameras and autograph books. Drinks were selling by the buckets. Meals were being ordered like it was a Friday night.

Then eight o'clock rolled around and an announcement came over the loud speaker, "Ladies and Gentlemen, Mr. John Wayne." Silence filled the room.

John was a good ole Kentucky farmer complete with bib overalls and a Massy Ferguson baseball cap. As soon as the crowd figured out what had happened, laughter filled the place. The owner ushered Mr. Wayne and his wife to their seats. Then people actually started asking Wayne for his autograph. Some patrons even asked to have their picture taken with him.

For a brief moment the owner thought that he was dead, but his patrons loved it and had a great time. And the owner had a good time at the bank the next day making the deposit. The only advertising he used was the readerboard.

One More Time

About five months later everything had died down about the promotion. The owner figured that everyone had forgotten about it completely. He was looking through the phone book again and came across a local gal by the name of Elizabeth Taylor. You guessed it, the next day, after a brief phone call, the sign went up: "Elizabeth Taylor To Dine Here Soon."

He was immediately besieged by phone calls asking him what he was trying to pull. The second time around it was not very successful at all. So if you want to try something like this, know that you can only get away with it once, and even then you'd better be real confident in your clientele so that you don't upset anyone.

We liked the idea so much that we wanted to recommend it to a client of ours in Fort Wayne. Obviously, John Wayne wouldn't work, and besides there was no John Wayne listed in the Fort Wayne phone book. But after an hour or so with it, we were able to find a Jimmy Carter, Jack Carter, two John Carsons, a Robert Conrad and a couple of William Conrads, John Winters, two Edward Alberts, a couple of

Richard Burtons, six Richard Harrises and 97 listings for Mr. Rogers! (Can you say, "Streetfighter"? I knew you could.)

A slight variation was used by a drugstore in a very small town in Louisiana. The type of town where if a person on one side of town sneezed, a person on the other end would yell, "Gesundheit."

This drugstore was going to experience some fierce competition for the first time. A major competitor was moving in. So the owner placed a sign out front that said simply, "We're Moving." It was hot news. Everyone was talking about it. The drugstore received phone calls from almost everyone in town asking if it were true. The owner would answer, "Sure are—moving our prices down!"

Don't Eat the Blue Snow

One really big attention-getter was a readerboard used by a small Italian restaurant during the winter after a large snowfall. Where the lot was plowed, there were large mounds of snow on either side of the entrance to the parking lot. Using green food coloring and water, the owner went outside with an old spray bottle and sprayed the snow green. It froze overnight. On the readerboard next to these mounds of green snow read, "Next year, let's ask for blue snow." It turned a lot of heads.

That's what you want to look for when looking at outdoor advertising—something that will say, "Hey, look at me."

Advertising Vehicle

Another source of inexpensive outdoor advertising is your own vehicle. At the very least you should be using a magnetic sign on each side so that as you and your people drive through town you can make some impressions.

One business in Chicago made a big impression with their delivery truck. Competitors would rib them about how small the company was. One day they got magnetic signs for the delivery van. Each sign contained the company name and address, but on the left side it read, "Delivery Vehicle #1." On the right side of the van it read, "Delivery Vehicle #2." On the back it read, "Delivery Vehicle #3." It drove the competition nuts.

They could have doubled the fleet by buying an alternate set of signs for delivery vehicle #4, 5, and 6, and changing signs every other week.

Actually, if you're going to number your vehicles, start with 7 or 9 or even 16. Don't start with 1. One is a lonely number. Seven, on the other hand, sounds like you can really give your customers the service.

When Business Is Dead

The type of vehicle you use can get attention, too. A bug exterminator named Mr. Bug uses an old hearse. Great attention-getter and probably cheap, too. How much demand can there be for old hearses?

That same idea could be used any number of ways. If your business has *doctor* in it, like Rug Doctor, an old ambulance would be great. A restaurant famous for hot chili or a Mexican restaurant with the hottest hot sauce in town surely could get some attention with an old fire truck. How about a team of male exotic dancers called U. S. Male. It's obvious that they should be driving around in an old Cushman three-wheeler they bought second-hand from the post office. Now, if only they thought it was a good idea.

Where to Park

If your truck or van has a good advertising paint job, make sure you park it in a high-visibility area. Don't hide it. Put it near the street where everyone can see it. Make an arrangement to park it in a parking lot of a major mall where everyone can see it. Don't let it go to waste. You might try to lease a parking space downtown to park it. Choose a spot by the street, preferably by an intersection where the truck can be easily noticed. (Don't use a parking garage for crying out loud.)

In Phoenix someone placed antique cars in high-visibility intersections and painted them with advertising messages. Great impact.

Trucks and vans might work out well if signage is strictly controlled in your area. The sign regs usually don't include vehicles. So buy one you can paint. It might not even have to have an engine in it. Be sure to read the ordinance very carefully first.

License to Steal

License plates are great advertising. Most states allow customized plates. With a car stuck behind you in traffic, a good customized license plate can make a great impact. A quick print shop in Tucson, Arizona, called AlphaGraphics uses Alpha-1, Alpha-2, Alpha-3, and so on. The manager of a health club has a plate that says, Get Fit. A bakery owners read, Bread. We like the idea so much we've seriously considered the thought of getting customized plates for our cars. Woody's will read "STREET" and Jeff's, "FIGHTER."

Anything Goes

When it comes to outdoor advertising, you can think way beyond the traditional forms like billboards. Look at your store. What would get passersby to glance over, take notice, and realize you're there? Earlier, we mentioned the Naked Furniture store that hired picketers to draw attention to the store. That's a form of nontraditional outdoor advertising. That's streetsmart outdoor advertising.

During the summer the karate school holds class on the parking lot. Get's a great deal of attention. Costs nothing. It probably gets the most attention when a class of 30 starts punching and kicking while giving a "kiai," which is a loud yell. If you were driving by, would you look over?

What could you do to get attention out in your parking lot, by the street? Could you do anything like Trevor True Value in Moline, Illinois? They held a fishing clinic. As part of the promotion, they got a local boat dealer to bring over some of his boats and display them in the parking lot. The dealer even contributed to the advertising of the program. Good attention-getter. Low cost.

There are all kinds of opportunities. Look. Think. Ask. Do.

11

EYES OPEN,
EARS TO THE GROUND

In the movie *Patton* starring George C. Scott, there's a memorable scene in which General Patton is about to do battle with Field Marshall Rommel for the first time. The night before the battle we see Patton in bed, reading. Leaning over to turn off the light, he places a book on the nightstand: *Tank Warfare* by Erwin Rommel.

The following morning the scene changes to the battlefield. Patton is looking at Rommel's advancing Panzers through his field glasses. The American tanks are well hidden under a ridge with plenty of camouflage as the Panzers creep closer and closer, the sounds of their metal tracks clanging and their diesel engines revving.

Then, as the suspense builds to where you can barely stand it, Patton gives the order to fire. And fire they do. Patton, still looking through his binoculars, sees that he's won an important victory against the foremost expert in tank warfare. As he looks at the defeated German tank corp, he screams with extreme excitement, "Rommel, you magnificent bastard . . . I read your book!"

Patton was obviously a streetfighter. Finding out all you can about a competitor can give you that little edge you need in developing an effective marketing program for your business. You'll probably find, however, that you won't be as fortunate as Patton in finding a book written about your competitor's business. Then again, many merchants are more than pleased to talk about their business, provided you ask them in the right way.

Streetsmart Research

Getting Your Competitors to Spill Their Guts

Make a list of questions that you would want to ask about a given competitor. Then get a young student to call them up posing as a marketing major at the local junior college. She should say that she is working on her thesis in the area of (your type of business). She then asks if it would be okay to ask a few questions.

If the manager or assistant manager is asked in the right manner, you'd be surprised at all the valuable information you can get.

Also, let that be a lesson to you. It's been our experience that too many merchants like to talk about their businesses. Without thinking, they'll tell a perfect stranger information they might not wish to tell their spouse, children, partner, or the IRS. It's not that they intentionally give out this information. A conversation may start about something totally nonrelated to their business. Most merchants are proud of their accomplishments, and rightfully so. They also like to talk too much and that's dangerous.

Giving a Brain Enema

A restaurant was worried sick about a competitor opening up down the street. The owner said that he would give anything to find out when they were going to open. We thought that was easy enough. The local directory assistance gave us the number, so we called up the soon-to-be new competitor. Once we got the soon-to-be new manager on the phone we told him, "My wife and I were looking forward to having a new restuarant in town. What kind of menu will you be having?" He told us. "When are you due to open?" He told us. "Will you be running any grand opening specials or any coupons?" He told us. We thanked him and wished him luck.

The client was amazed and relieved at our little technique. It made his job a lot easier in coming up with a competitive entry strategy to combat this new competitor.

But the brain-enema king has to be one of our *Streetfighter* subscribers in Columbus, Ohio. He was intrigued by the marketing and operations program used by the local franchisee of a major national restaurant. He contacted the assistant manager of the place and told him he thought their restaurant was doing a tremendous job. He then actually talked the assistant manager into meeting him so they could talk further.

At the meeting he pulled out a tape recorder and started asking some very revealing questions about their operation. This assistant manager told all.

We have on a number of occasions gone to a competitor of a client, posing as a customer, and by asking a few questions and shooting the breeze for an hour, been able to extract very valuable information. In one such situation we acted as if we couldn't believe that they could possibly do the volume the manager told us they did. He was ready to pull out the P&L statement to prove it to us!

Profits Down the Drain

The owner of one of the nightclubs mentioned in an earlier chapter had a couple of techniques he used to monitor what his competition was doing. The first was asking his suppliers, who were more than happy to tell him what his competition ordered. He also reasoned that if he could get this information, so could his competitors.

Then he approached the route man who serviced the cigarette machines. He noticed that the dollar volume of the cigarette machines would go up or down in proportion to the total dollar volume of his club. He figured that probably would be the case for his competitors as well. So he got the route man to give him a weekly total of all the money taken out of the cigarette machines of those clubs where they had machines.

Perhaps one of the more interesting approaches he took was to visit the other clubs in person. Just because there was a crowd, or the lack of one, didn't necessarily mean they were making money. It all depended on whether the customers were drinking heavily or not.

To get an indication, he merely went into the restroom. If there was a waiting line to use the facilities, he knew they were drinking a lot and the club was making money. But, if the bathroom was vacant, their business might just be ready to go down the sewer.

Self-Analysis

Doing it to yourself is just as important as to your competition. Even more so. Where are your customers coming from? Why do they come to you? Do they buy elsewhere? How did they hear about you? What does the public think about your operation? What radio station do they listen to?

All of these questions can be answered with some simple streetwise research techniques that you can do yourself. The first approach is called a "scattergram," and will tell you where your customers are coming from and, more important, where they're not.

The Triple-A Scattergram Plan

The three A's stand for Ascertain, Analyze, and Act.

Ascertain

First you need the addresses of your customers. This will tell you exactly where they live. A mailing list, if you have one, can give you that information. If you don't have one, you can run a free drawing contest like the one described in Chapter 6.

Once you've either located or compiled your list of customers, get a wall map of your city. On the map, using straight pins with large, round heads, plot the addresses from the list.

This can be a time-consuming project, so one smart merchant hired an off-duty cab driver to come in and do the plotting for them. It took the cabby less than an hour for the entire job.

After all the addresses have been plotted, you'll begin to see that the pins begin to form a pattern. Step back. See where your concentration of customers are. Also, look to see where the concentration of customers *isn't*. Why not?

Analyze

There could be a number of reasons for this dropout. You might have a major competitor in that area or a natural barrier that divides you from those potential customers. For example, if there's a bridge, four-lane highway, or railroad track to cross to get to your store, many people won't do it. It's a subconscious behavior, but it does exist.

Another reason for a section of the map to be void of pins is because it's a nonresidential area. A park or a lake would also fall into this category, and unless you have a target audience that consists of squirrels or mermaids, you really shouldn't worry about this area.

Act

Use everything you have at your disposal to promote trial among those residents who aren't your customers. Cross-promotions, door hangers, direct mail, and community-involvement programs can all help to bring some of those people to your store. Since they are presently not your customers, you might want to consider a higher-liability discount to make their first visit that much more attractive.

I'm New in Town

To get an indication of what people think about your business, go to an area where many of your target audience might be hanging out. This was done by a stereo dealer who visited a video arcade. He'd approach a quarterless Pac Man junkie and tell him or her, "I'm new in town and I need to get some new stereo equipment. Where's a decent place to go?"

They'd tell him, and in many cases his store wasn't mentioned. If it wasn't, he then would say, "I noticed (insert name of store) the other day. Are they any good?" That way he found out what their impression was of his store. In that case he found out that many people felt his store was higher priced than most of the others but that it carried top-quality stereo gear. With that information he was able to come up with a campaign to correct that misconception in the buying public's mind.

If you're well known in your community, find a friend to do it for you. Or agree to change cities for a day with a merchant in another city to help each other out.

After talking to a couple dozen people, you should begin to see a pattern that could give you some very valuable insight. Granted, this is not going to give you hard information with a minute margin for error, but it will give you an indication. Perhaps it will confirm a suspicion you've had about your business. It also won't cost you an arm and leg, either.

What's Your favorite Radio Station?

A car dealership wanted to find out what radio stations their customers listen to. To get a rough idea, they had the mechanics keep a log of every car that came in for service as to which station the car radio was tuned to when it was brought in.

They also made a notation if it was a new or used car. Plus, they were even able to figure out if a certain station would be best for selling a specific model.

The same idea was used by an independent garage and a car wash. A slight variation was used by a stereo dealer when tuners were brought in for repair.

You might not be able to see what a customer's radio is tuned to, but there is a way to find out how they heard about you. Ask them. If someone calls your store for information, the last thing you should do before you hang up is ask, "By the way, how did you hear about us?" It's so simple and will give some indication as to what advertising programs are bringing you some action.

Competitive Entry Strategies

Almost every business is experiencing more and more competition. It comes from major chains or franchises. It comes from the Ma-and-Pa shops. It comes from the regional level and it comes and it comes and it comes. What do you do with a new kid in town? Play dead until after they've had their grand opening? Wrong! That's exactly what most merchants do. They wait, figuring there's nothing they can do to hurt the opening of a new store. People love something new and will flock to a new place for awhile. Then things seem to level off.

A video store in Denver, Colorado, was scared when a new competitor was going to open up down the street. Worse, the competitor was spending a small fortune in the newspaper, on TV, and on radio announcing the grand opening. The owner of the video store was very concerned, but then he had a brainstorm.

On the day of the competitor's grand opening, our streetsmart merchant flew a helium-filled miniature blimp about his own store. A few balloons and pennants to dress up the front of the store, and on the readerboard outside it said, "Now Open." (Note that it didn't say "Grand Opening.")

Half of the would-be competitor's customers accidently went to the wrong store. He, of course, honored all the competition's coupons that day and priced all his merchandise accordingly. It was the best ad campaign he'd ever had. The cost? How much is a little hot air?

Steal a Grand, Save $41,600

That technique probably had another benefit that its inventor never thought of. Many new businesses, especially national chains, have yearly expectations from a new store, often based on the percentage of the grand opening. In the food service industry, it's often expected that a store will settle in at about 80 percent of the grand opening level.

For example, if a restaurant opens its first month with an average weekly take of $10,000, then they'll expect that store to settle in at an average of about $8000. But if you can lower the opening sales, you can then lower their expectations.

If a store makes a great deal less than expected, it puts up a red flag to management. It's a sore spot that they'll spend a great deal of time to correct. But if you could steal $1000 a week at the opener, that particular unit won't be expected to do as well. Instead of opening at $10,000, it opens at $9000. When you back off the 80 percent, it should settle in at $7200 a week, not $8000. That's $41,600 a year in sales they won't be missing as much.

Stealing away that $1000 a week is going to take some work. It means that you have to pull out all the stops. Use everything you've got. Direct mail, community involvement, or bounce-back coupons in the store. This is one time where you forget the "one at a time, one week at a time" rule for cross promotions. Set a couple up right in their own back yard.

Frequency promotions will also work well against a grand opening. This is where you provide your customers with a punch card or certificate every time they buy from you. When they buy five, they get the sixth one free. Start the promotion four weeks in front of the competitor's grand opening, if possible. They'll be so close to getting a free one, that your customers might just wait a few weeks before giving your competitor a try.

The Vertical Smorgasbord

Another great way to kill a competitor's grand opening is with the vertical smorgasbord. It's also a tremendous turnaround vehicle.

We first discovered the vertical smorgasbord concept when it was used by a restaurant. Since then we've been able to apply the same concept to a number of different types of merchants.

The smorgasbord itself is simple. For one day you offer a certain type of merchandise or food item at a ridiculously low price. All the pizza you can eat for 99 cents blew the door off.

This type of promotion lines people up for hours. They'll come out of the woodwork if the deal is good enough. Keep in mind, the promotion itself isn't necessarily a profit-maker, though it can be. The main point is to let people know you exist.

If you've just taken over an operation with a very poor reputation in town, it often seems to take forever before you begin to build the confidence of the community. The smorgasbord will allow you to get them to try you at least one more time.

Aside from 99 cents for all the pizza you can eat, it's been done with 29-cent tacos, 20-cent hamburgers, free beer and wine, $2.99 prime rib dinner, 19-cent cross-stich floss, 1-cent photocopies, and a one-free-month membership at a karate school.

In addition to the price point being one of the magic elements, the length of the promotion is equally important. It's only one day, two at the most.

This is also a way to end a price war. That's why the 19-cent floss smorgasbord was used. The regular price was 39 cents. Then a competitor tried to capture a larger share of the market by dropping his price a penny. Other places responded by dropping their price two pennies. The way it was going, eventually nobody would make money on this.

To solve this problem, the streetsmart owner of a fabric and yarn shop had a two-day promotion in which people could buy floss at 19 cents. This was almost as little as her competitors were paying for it. Since she was going to order such a large quantity for this promotion, she was able to negotiate a good price that allowed her to make a decent profit even at this ridiculously low price.

She not only preempted all her competitor's prices, but she flooded the market with the product. Since the price was so low, cross-stich enthusiasts stocked up with a six-month supply of the many hundreds of different colors. After her promotion, the floss business was very slow for months.

This wasn't just a free-for-all. It was a carefully planned promotion. She had plenty of other activities going on to make this a special event, including a good inventory of regularly priced merchandise.

The Ten Commandments of Vertical Smorgasbords

1. Be prepared. Have plenty of the sale merchandise on hand. Running out can really upset the people.

2. Have plenty of help. You'll need all your employees to help with this one. One should do nothing but answer the phones. See if your dealer reps will help you out too.

3. Don't advertise too far in advance. Three or four days in front of the promotion should be sufficient. As soon as you announce this promotion, provided you've done your homework, it could kill sales until the promotion. Also, you don't want to give your competition any more advance warning than you have to.

A competitor may get much of your overflow. Some have even called to give their thanks for the business. But since competitors weren't prepared, most of the people who went to them had a very poor experience.

4. Don't advertise too much. This shouldn't be an advertising-intensive program provided you've picked the right price point. Promote it internally and on your readerboard. A couple of small ads in the newspaper, maybe some door hangers. Direct mail may be too risky with this tight a time period.

5. Provide your customers with a bounce-back coupon. They've been to your store under a very unique situation. You now want to get them back

under more normal conditions. The coupon could be something on the order of, "Thank you for coming to our party. We'd like to see you again."

6. This should be a big party. You might include balloons, music, prizes, jugglers, clowns, the local high school marching band. Make it fun.

7. Create a good reason for the promotion. Store anniversary is always a good one. No matter how insignificant the reason for the promotion may sound, it will add to the credibility if you have some kind of reason for this party.

8. If you have a few locations, hold the promotion in only one of them. Many people will stop by and see the waiting line. Once they've got your name, your product, your service in their minds, they often will go to the other side of town to the other location and pay full price.

9. Don't add extra space or seating. Part of the fun and excitement is the crowded effect. This is particularly important for restaurants. If you had a tent outside with extra seating, and were providing an "all you can" type of smorg, your food cost would be astronomical. With regular seating, on the other hand, the crowds waiting in line will make most people feel that they should give someone else a chance.

10. Spend some time with your staff to do a post-smorg analysis. What did you do right? What could be improved if you did it again? Play "what if." What if we increased the price by ten cents, or a dollar? What if we ran it for two days instead of one? What if we had a radio remote? What if we added a few other products or took away a few of the products?

You don't want to do this too often, otherwise it will lose its dramatic effct. But, it can be repeated, and every time you do, you should be making those small improvements.

Creative Ignorance

Creative Ignorance is one of the more subtle philosophies of a streetfighter. You've read a number of examples of creative ignorance throughout this book, but it's a principle worthy of development. It can be used in almost any aspect of advertising, promotions, marketing, or really any part of running a small business.

An example: There was this very small ladies' apparel shop that opened up in a downtown area. The owner couldn't afford to do much advertising. As a matter of fact, the only thing she could afford to do was print up a few thousand fliers.

Now she had to get these fliers into the hands of the people who would most likely buy from her. She couldn't afford to mail them, so she determined that the only way she could distribute them was to deliver them herself. This wasn't a difficult task because she was near a number of large office buildings.

But when she entered the first building, fliers in hand, she noticed a rather large sign making it quite clear that there was no soliciting allowed. She thought for a moment, then went inside and started delivering the fliers office by office, floor by floor.

About half-way up the first building, a security guard informed her that she couldn't do that. He made reference to the sign downstairs that strictly forbids soliciting. She immediately apologized, saying, "I'm sorry, I didn't know." She left immediately.

Then on to the next building she went, ignoring the same type of sign. After that, there were many more buildings, each having a similar sign. In some buildings she was asked to leave right away. In some she got part of the way through before being asked to vacate. In others she made it all the way through without attracting any attention.

She delivered hundreds of fliers that day. It didn't cost her a thing to distribute her fliers. She knew there were signs there. But, she also knew that the worst thing that would happen to her is that she would be asked to leave. That's a pretty low risk with the possibility of a high reward.

The same idea could be used when placing fliers on car windshields in parking lots. If you're asked to quit, you do so and leave immediately. If no one bothers you, go about your work. A little common sense is all that's needed. You might think twice about placing fliers on staff cars in a parking lot for the CIA, especially if their guards carry automatic weapons and use Dobermans, but the YMCA across the street—now that's a different story.

It's a game. You use creative ignorance when you negotiate with media salespeople. Creative ignorance is buying a porta-sign to help the local Boy Scouts sell Christmas trees on your parking lot even though there's a city ordinance against these signs. Creative ignorance is videotaping "General Hospital" and showing it on the large-screen TV in your bar until you get a telegram from ABC telling you to quit or else. Creative ignorance is one facet of streetfighting.

Conclusion

A streetfighter is a special person, one who is willing to grasp for everything in reach and then some. Streetfighting is more than specific advertising techniques or marketing programs. If anything, we want you to understand that it's the attitude of a streetfighter that makes for outstanding accomplishments. Reading this book will not make you a streetfighter, but we hope it will give you some guidance on how you can take your natural abilities and apply them to your bottom line.

Being a streetfighter is special. A streetfighter is a member of an elite group of small business people who outthink their competition rather than outspend them. It's brains over bucks, mind over money. It's Main Street, not Madison Avenue, and it might just be the ticket to help you put your business on the road to bigger profits.

INDEX